The Outrageous Myths
of E

The Outrageous Myths of Enlightenment

Stephen Wingate

Atma Publishing

Atma Publishing
www.AtmaPublishing.com

The Outrageous Myths of Enlightenment
Copyright © Stephen Wingate 2006
www.LivingInPeace-TheNaturalState.com
First Printing: August 2006

All rights reserved. No part of this publication may be reproduced or transmitted in any form or by any means, electronic or mechanical, including photocopying, recording or by any information or retrieval system without written permission by the publisher, except for the inclusion of brief quotations in a review.

ISBN 0-9787254-0-9

Printed in the USA by Morris Publishing
3212 E. Hwy 30
Kearney, NE 68847
800-650-7888

Cover Design © Morris Publishing 2006

Contents

Preface	xi
Foreword	xii
Introduction	xiii

Part I Writings

1.	Bottom Line: How Does This Work?	15
2.	Reflections	17
3.	When I Am Born	20
4.	Waiting	21
5.	A Zen Student's Story	21

Part II Correspondence & Dialogues

1.	Here's Where I Get Pissed Off	22
2.	False Expectations	23
3.	Which is the True Mystical Experience?	24
4.	I Feel I May Need a Teacher	26
5.	There's a Screaming Contradiction!	27
6.	Isn't This Just Another Doing?	28
7.	Just Another Term for Enlightenment?	29
8.	What Can I Expect to Get Out of This?	30
9.	Medical Doctors, Psychologists, and Psychiatrists	32
10.	But I Am a Separate Person: I Am Not You!	32
11.	The Never-Ending Nightmare	34
12.	Emotional Detachment and Control	35
13.	Show Me This Nothing	36
14.	Suffering Over the Suffering of Others	38
15.	I Need to be Guided Home	39
16.	But There is Still the Appearance of 'I'	41
17.	Liberation From the Mind	42
18.	Egoic Interactions and Confrontations	43
19.	Love and Intimate Relationships	43
20.	I Feel Absolutely Worthless	45
21.	Permanent States?	46
22.	I Disagree With Everything You're Saying	47
23.	How Do I See This For Myself?	49
24.	Make This Observation	51
25.	Ramana Maharshi Said	54

26. Mental Chatter and Flailing About	55
27. Everything Else is Irrelevant	56
28. Meeting With a Teacher	58
29. Frustration and a Yearning to Know	60
30. Questions Everywhere But Not a Drop of Peace	61
31. How Do I Get Off the Merry-Go-Round?	62
32. Why is It So Difficult to Wake Up?	63
33. Is There a Natural Progression?	64
34. The Recognition is Not Happening	66
35. How Do You Get Beyond the Mind?	67
36. Give Yourself Two Weeks	68
37. Keep Asking Questions Until They're Burned Away	70
38. What's Holding You Back From Seeing This?	72
39. Death and Reincarnation	73
40. Awareness is the I AM THAT I AM	75
41. Sidetracked by the Inessentials	76
42. Is There Free Will or Does Destiny Rule?	77
43. Why the Doubts?	79
44. This Koan Called Advaita	80
45. Is Psychological Suffering Just a Bad Idea?	83
46. Agnosticism: The One True Faith?	84
47. Panic Attacks	86
48. Attention vs. Awareness	87
49. Fed-Up with Seeking!	88
50. Any Additional Pointers?	89
51. From Concepts to Living Experience	90
52. Witness the Dissolution of the 'I'	91
53. How Will I Know the Understanding is Complete?	94
54. Fear of Letting Go of the Mind	96
55. Since I am Not the Body, Should I Maintain It?	98
56. Drop the Tools Into the Tool Shed	99
57. I'd Like to Wake Up and Say, 'A-ha!'	102
58. I Often Forget Who I Am	103
59. The Burning Desire to Know Who I Am	105
60. Your Will is the Will of the Universe	109
61. This is the Peace That's at Peace with War	109
62. The So-Called Sage Knows He is Powerless	112
63. Going to Battle with an Unloaded Weapon	113
64. How's the Weather?	114
65. The Recognition Brought on a Sense of Peace	116
66. Something Strange is Happening Here!	117

67. There Was a Seeing that There's Nobody Home	118
68. Nothing Mystical—Nothing Mundane	120
69. It's 4:00am: Do You Know the Source of Suffering?	121
70. Ten Days to Realize This: I Exist!	122
71. I'm Being Moved Around Like a Puppet	123
72. How Did the Suffering Return?	125
73. The Pointers Found Fertile Ground	126
74. A Grenade Has Gone Off in the Brain!	128
75. Why am I Here? What's the Purpose?	129
76. Don't Use Any Words—Now Tell Me What's Left?	131
77. Words Imply Duality Where None Exists	133
78. Happiness and Sadness: Are They Just Energy?	134
79. The Key to Resolving Your Self-Inquiry	135
80. This Puppet Has Eyes to See and Ears to Hear	136
81. You Can't Wake Up—You Were Never Asleep	138
82. Am I in Awareness or is Awareness in Me?	139
83. All Questions Dissolve in This 'Not Knowing'	141
84. Singing to the Choir: The Bullshit Song	143
85. Who Sets the Intention to be Free of Seeking?	144
86. How Does This Help Me Cope with My Life?	145
87. I Don't Need to Look for the Truth Anymore	146
88. How Do You Know You're Not Already Awake?	149
89. I Don't Want to Drop My Story!	153
90. I Can Feel That This is Working	154
91. Seeking a Spiritual Cure Fuels the Fire of Suffering	156
92. Your Search is Done	157
93. You and Me Are the Same One: This is Love	159
94. Does This Understanding Not Include God?	163
95. I Can't Deny That Everything is Simply Happening	164
96. Look Away from the Stories and Let Them Be	166
97. I'm Waiting for a Radical or Sudden Shift	167
98. No Separate I—No Suffering—No Awakening	168
99. Is There Any Awakening or Liberation?	170
100. That Kundalini Energy Came Up: It Scared Me	171
101. The Resolution of Seeking and Suffering	172
102. Why Am I Still Seeking?	174
103. It is Done!	175
104. The Concept of Liberation is Another Golden Carrot	177
105. Watching the Snow Fall	178
106. I Don't Know What Awareness Is	179
107. Can There Be Any Mistakes?	180

108.	All I Can Say Is 'I Don't Know'	181
109.	I Am the Beginning and End of All Suffering	183
110.	I Cant Get Past the Sense That I Am This Body/Brain	185
111.	I AM: Everything Else is Imagination	188
112.	I Feel Like an Alien	188
113.	It Really is This Simple, Isn't It	190
114.	Waiting for the Explosive Moment of Realization	192
115.	Give it Up and Go Wash the Dishes	193
116.	Stuck on a Hamster Wheel	196
117.	You Are the 'Watching'—So Just Watch	198
118.	Are Experiences Personal or Impersonal?	199
119.	Years of Searching and Struggling Have Evaporated	200
120.	Ending Psychological Suffering is Shockingly Simple	201
121.	Where Does All of This Leave Me?	204

Preface

My intense search for Peace started in my early twenties and lasted for over twenty years. The desire to know and experience the truth that the ancient traditions were pointing to led me down many paths. I studied most of the Eastern and Western religious philosophies and some of the non-mainstream approaches as well. I felt a strong resonance with the non-dual philosophies as presented in Christian Mysticism, Zen Buddhism, Taoism, and Advaita-Vedanta.

In 1998 I discovered the book *I AM THAT* by Nisargadatta Maharaj and began reading it. Immediately there was an intuitive, powerfully intense feeling that this man understands the truth that the ancient traditions were pointing to, and more importantly, he was *living* this truth! His words are alive and struck me to the core of my being. I had to come to this understanding myself, somehow, someway.

After years of reading and re-reading the book, I felt I had a strong intellectual understanding of the truth that Nisargadatta was pointing to, but it wasn't my *living* experience. This led to a sense of terrible frustration. I felt I needed to find someone who was living this truth and was able to help me make it my daily, living experience.

In 2004 I learned of a man called 'Sailor' Bob Adamson from Australia who was a student of Nisargadatta Maharaj and who has been helping others come to the understanding for over twenty-nine years. Bob led me to his student, John Wheeler, from Santa Cruz, California who is also sharing this message in the same tradition. I met John Wheeler in 2004. Through this meeting and our conversations that followed, the intellectual understanding has become my living experience.

After more than twenty years of struggling and searching for Peace, the seeking has come to an end. I am thankful to Nisargadatta Maharaj, 'Sailor' Bob Adamson, and John Wheeler who pointed me to the Peace that I already was and always have been.

Stephen Wingate
Boston, Massachusetts, USA
June 2006

Foreword

This book provides a wealth of extremely clear, direct and practical pointers that lay bare the root causes of our suffering, and point the way to life free of psychological suffering. With insight, clarity, patience, compassion and humor, Stephen reminds us again and again that the only thing that can cause us suffering is thinking and imagination based on our presumed existence as separate individuals.

As he clearly shows, one's true nature is not a separate individual at all. There is no controlling entity behind our thoughts, feelings, perceptions and actions. In direct looking, we discover ourselves to be that clear, open and spacious presence of awareness in which all appearances spontaneously arise and set.

Stephen has a wonderful gift of sharing these insights, which are based on his own clear and solid experience. His words carry the fragrance of peace and clarity to which they point. The writings and dialogues in this book will undermine any residual doubts, questions and caveats raised by the mind and leave you in your natural state of joyful awareness.

John Wheeler

Introduction

What are Self-realization, Awakening, Liberation, and Enlightenment?

You are the One Self, Awareness Itself. Stop for a moment right now, and notice the presence of awareness that you are—here and now. Notice that you are spacious, open, awake and free. Notice that these words are arising in this spacious openness that you are. Notice that all of the activities of the mind, the seeking and suffering, the resistance and attachments, the stories and dramas all play out in you—this spacious, open presence of awareness.

This peaceful, loving, spacious openness is what you are. This spacious openness is the Self, the Liberation, the Awakening, the Enlightenment, the Peace and the Love for which you've been seeking. You have always been, and always will be simply THIS.

It's apparent that you already are this witnessing presence; you are the Self. You know this from your own direct experience. Everywhere you go; there you are as this witnessing presence. Right now you are this freedom, this liberation, this awakening, this enlightenment. There is nothing mystical about your presence as awareness—you just are. Notice it now.

There can be a tendency to 'spiritualize' or 'mystify' this simple presence of awareness that is always here and now, especially after having what could be called life-changing experiences, realizations and epiphanies. You are always this simple witnessing presence. Sometimes you witness what seem to be mystical experiences, and other times the mundane, but you are always this simple witnessing presence—peaceful and free.

All there is, is This—there's nothing else.
There's nowhere to go, nothing to do, nothing to become.
This is all there is.
All there ever was is This.
All there ever will be is This.
There is nothing else—just This.
Nothing mystical. Nothing mundane.
Just This.
And You are This.

My interest in communicating this message is to de-mystify the concepts of Awakening, Liberation, Self-realization, and Enlightenment. And to share the fact that it's possible to be free of psychological suffering, and free of spiritual seeking.

My approach is to share my direct experience, and to speak from the heart about what I have found to be true. And I'm finding that those who stop for a moment, consider the suggestions offered, and apply them to their own direct experience are finding themselves free of psychological suffering and spiritual seeking.

You may notice that the message being shared here is shockingly simple. And possibly for that reason, those who have keenly developed intellects tend to overlook the obvious, and continue exercising their intellect with never-ending questions, doubts, and 'Yes, buts!' So the appearance of suffering and seeking goes on.

If you stop for a few moments and look to your own direct experience for the answers, you may be surprised how quickly and easily psychological suffering and spiritual seeking come to an end. If your interest is in being free of psychological suffering and free of the outrageous myths of enlightenment, then look to your own direct experience for answers to the fundamental questions posed here. It is this simple.

Being free of psychological suffering and spiritual seeking does not require years of spiritual practice, meditation, faith, trust, understanding of complex religious philosophies, or a keenly developed intellect. Psychological suffering and your spiritual search come to an end by seeing in your own direct experience that what you are in essence is simply awareness, and that nothing can trouble you but imagination.

Stephen Wingate

Part I Writings

1

Bottom Line: How Does This Work?

There is nothing mystical or magical about this. It is simple, logical and applicable to everyone. This is not just for special beings who were able to transcend their earthly fetters, and rise above the lowly egoic peasantry through years of self-sacrifice and meditation. That's all nonsense. This is true for anyone and everyone. These words apply to you and to me:

'We are free here and now, it is only the mind that imagines bondage. Seeing that there is no such thing as a permanent, separate person, all becomes clear. You are the immensity and infinity of consciousness. It is lucid, silent, peaceful, alert, and unafraid—without desire and fear. To realize this is the end of all seeking'.
Nisargadatta Maharaj

These few words say it all. Let's break them down.

1. *'We are free here and now, it is only the mind that imagines bondage'.*

Is this true? Consider your own experience. When you are sitting quietly, not thinking about yourself and your problems, can anything trouble you? Can there be any bondage if you are not imagining yourself to be bound? Of course you are free here and now! Nisargadatta puts it another way, too: *'Nothing can trouble you but your own imagination'.* There is no such thing as bondage. It is merely a concept!

2. *'Seeing that there is no such thing as a permanent, separate person, all becomes clear'.*

Is this true? Look for yourself. What is the common denominator in all of your suffering, all of your problems? What is at the center of your life situation? What is this 'me' that says, 'my' life, 'my' problems? If it is seen that there is no separate me, no separate person here at all, can there be any suffering? The 'me' who was bound and suffering is just imagination. Reading the words and agreeing or disagreeing is not enough. Seeing this for yourself is the key.

3. *'You are the immensity and infinity of consciousness. It is lucid, silent, peaceful, alert, and unafraid—without desire and fear'.*

If I am not the separate person I thought I was then what am I? Isn't consciousness your essential nature? If you are not conscious can anything else exist? Can there be a 'me' and 'my' story if consciousness is not there to witness it? What is the nature of pure consciousness? Isn't it clear, silent, peaceful, alert, unafraid? So consciousness is what you are: not a separate person.

4. *'To realize this is the end of all seeking'.*

For what are you seeking? Aren't you seeking for clarity, peace, freedom from desire and fear? Aren't these the characteristics of consciousness? You are what you are seeking! Realizing that you are consciousness, not the separate person you imagined yourself to be, the seeking comes to an end and you are free!

When these words are understood and known as the truth they become your daily living experience. It's as simple as it looks. There's nothing magical or mystical about it. There is no need for any mystical experience of universal love and union. The understanding brings on a simple experience of Peace and well-being that is felt as the common ground of all your daily experiences. Happiness and sadness, laughter and tears, anger and joy: all come and go in this awareness of peace and well-being. Nothing to gain. Nothing to lose. Everything is as it is.

2

Reflections

What do you want ultimately? What is real? What is imagination?

Imagination can be seen. Can what is real be seen? <u>Is imagination troubling you? Do you take images to be real and run from them or long after them?</u>

Awareness is the ultimate context of all existence. Not an idea of awareness, but awareness itself, yourself. What is aware of being here and reading these words right now? Stop. What is it that stopped? What is here before, during, and after what stopped? You are not what stopped. You cannot begin. You cannot stop.

You are this awareness, now. You are always this awareness. This awareness is life itself. You don't *have* a life; you *are* life. You cannot *attain* eternal life; you *are* eternal life. All there is, is eternal life, this awareness, and you are This.

Truth is the infinite, absolute context in which everything is born, lives, and dies. This truth is what you are. This awareness is what you are. You are This.

When the thought 'I' arises and is identified with a body and mind, this is the birth of separation, conflict, struggle, and death. You are not the sensations of the body or the thoughts of the mind. What is real? What is imagination? The body and mind can be seen, felt, and experienced. Can what is real be seen, felt, and experienced? Is the seer real? Is the seen real? Is the seeing real? What is real? What is imagination?

'I am' the beginning and end of all trouble, all suffering. What is born and what dies? Death happens to something that was born. Were you ever born? When the thought 'I' is born the world is born. Before the thought 'I' is born, all is. No 'I', no world. The thought 'I' is a picture projected onto a screen. The screen is you, awareness. Without you, there is no 'I' and no world. You are the projector, the projecting, the screen and the projections. Without you, awareness, nothing is.

What is imagination? What is real? Look now! What is the common denominator in all your troubles, all your suffering? Is it you, the 'me', the 'I' you call yourself? What is this 'I'? Is it real? Is it imagination? When the 'I' is known to be imagination what happens to all your troubles, all your suffering? When the 'I' is known to be imagination, what happens to the world?

As trouble is experienced, as suffering is experienced, if you ask, 'Who is suffering?' What will be found? Who is reading these words right now? When the 'I' is seen to be imagination, what's left? You are! Awareness is! Home is awareness. Home is peace. Home is heaven. All paths to heaven lead to hell.

The doer is the I-image, the 'me', and is unreal (having no independent, permanent existence), it is imaginary. All is happening. Who is the doer? What is imagination? What is real? Do look, now.

Happiness and sadness, right and wrong, good and bad: how are they born? When are they born? What is the context into which they are born? There is laughter. There are tears. Is there any difference to you? What is it that says, 'good'? What is it that says, 'bad'? What is classification, judgment, and knowledge? Is it thought? Is it thinking?

Awareness is not a thought. Thoughts happen in awareness. Thinking is division, separation, conflict—me/not me, good/bad, like/dislike.

There are pleasurable sensations felt as the body. There are painful sensations felt as the body. The objects of pleasure are remembered and sought. The objects of pain are remembered and shunned. Pain happens now and is real now. Pleasure happens now and is real now. Pain and pleasure are not a problem. Suffering is different.

Desire is the memory of pleasure. Fear is the memory of pain. Suffering is desire and fear: 'I want', and 'I don't want'. What is desired is a memory. What is feared is a memory. Memories are images, imagination. Imagination is not real. What is real? What is imagination? Do you see it now? Is it clear?

What is desired? Ultimately, isn't desire the desire for love, peace, happiness, union: the desire for Being? What is feared? Ultimately, isn't fear the fear of conflict, war, suffering, dissolution: the fear of not Being? Is it possible for you to 'not be'? What is it that can 'be' and then 'not be'?

There is this absolute, infinite, undivided awareness until the first thought is born: the thought 'I'. When the I-thought is born, the world is born. The world is 'not I'. The I-thought is the birth of fear and desire. Before I am, All Is. Who is there to have fear and desire before I am? Truly, what I AM is before, during, and after the arising of the I-thought. Are there any words for it? The body is a flowing series of sensations. The mind is a flowing series of images. What is witnessing these sensations and images? What is witnessing this body and mind? You are. Who are you?

Is there time without imagination? Are memories what is? Are memories the future? There are images and sensations. Is there a real entity called me? Space and time are thoughts, images, concepts, past, present, future. All of these are the same. They are all relative and they have no separate, independent existence, no absolute reality.

All exists now. All there is, is now. All there is, is the all. The all and the now is the real. The thinking process, which is the mind, divides the all into the many, divides the now into the past and future. The division of the all into the many, and the now into the past and future is imagination. Imagination is not the real. What is imagination? Look now.

If some 'thing' is seen, is it real? Seeing some 'thing' implies division, which implies naming, which implies recognizing, which implies the past, which implies time, which implies thought. Can we see without dividing, without naming, without recognizing, without the past, without time, without thought? Seeing some 'thing' implies a seer, the seen and seeing. What is imagination? What is real? Feel it?

Intelligence is life itself, awareness. Can awareness see all that is, as it is, now? Can we see as intelligence sees and not as thought sees? Can we see what *is* rather than what *was*? Can we see what is real rather than what is imagined?

When we see all as it is now, what is there to fear? *Who* is to be afraid? There is desire: 'I want'. There is fear: 'I don't want'. Every 'thing' you desire is imaginary. Every 'thing' you fear is imaginary. The 'you' that wants and fears is imaginary.

Before 'I am' is reality. After 'I am' is imagination. 'I' is imagination. All is real.

Ultimately, what I want is what I AM: Awareness, Love, Happiness, Peace, Unity, Heaven.

When I Am Born

When I am born
You are born
I can never be one with you

When we are born
They are born
We can never be one with them

Is there any surprise
That frustration should arise
When trying to make two become one?

Before I am
Is before you are
Before two
There is one

Before we are
Is before they are
Before us and them is one

Before I am
All is I AM
Not even one

What is this I that is born?

4

Waiting

Are you waiting for something to happen?
This is it!
There's nothing else!
Nothing to gain.
Nothing to lose.
This is all there is.
Are you still waiting?
This is it, really.
Just this.

5

A Zen Student's Story

When will the penny drop?
I asked my Zen master that question. I said, 'Master, when did the penny drop for you?'
The Zen master crowed, 'Just now!'
Damn it! I was extremely disappointed because I'd been following his guidance for several years, and he was admitting he just now became enlightened!
One year later I still hadn't gotten it, so I asked another question: 'Master, when will the penny drop for me?'
The Zen master shouted angrily, 'Just now! God damn it, JUST NOW!'
And BANG! The penny dropped!
My eyes sparkled and opened wide, and with a great big glowing smile, I said, 'Thank you, master, NOW I get it!'
And here I AM.

Part II Correspondence & Dialogues

1

Here's Where I Get Pissed Off

Question: I've been on this spiritual search for over thirty years now. I've read just about every book by every author ever written. I've read Ramana Maharshi, Nisargadatta, Krishnamurti, Eckhart Tolle, the Bible, the Buddhist scriptures and on and on. I've been to so many spiritual retreats and met with so many teachers and so called gurus that it makes me nauseous just thinking about it. There are times when I feel like it's all a bunch of nonsense. Several times through the years I've thrown away all my books and given up. But I feel like something keeps pulling me back into the spiritual search and here I am again. It seems like my suffering pulls me back into the spiritual seeking, and the seeking keeps the suffering going.

Stephen: I know the feeling. The good news is the searching can come to an end. You can throw away all of your books and be done with it. You don't need another thirty years of searching and suffering. In your last sentence you said, 'It seems like my suffering pulls me back into the spiritual seeking and the seeking keeps the suffering going'. This is exactly the case, isn't it? The seeking is the suffering. So what are you seeking? What can you get that will satisfy this seeking and end the suffering?

Q: I don't even know what I want anymore. At this point I'm happy with just a few minutes of peace. There seems to be a few minutes each day that there is no internal struggle going on, no seeking, and in these moments I feel at peace. I'm fed up with this struggling. It seems to be never ending. I'm tired.

S: So you've seen clearly that the seeking is the suffering, and that when there is no seeking there is peace.

Q: Yes, of course, but this peace is short-lived. I want it to be, as you say, 'my daily living experience'.

S: Have you gotten to the root of the matter and found out who is seeking? Who wants to experience peace? Who is tired? Who is this 'me' that you call yourself?

Q: You know, here's where I get pissed off. I love all of this Advaita, non-duality talk, I really do. But when I hear this question over and over again it makes me sick. Please don't go there. I tried the Ramana Maharshi approach, 'Who am I? Who am I? Who am I?'—Ad nauseum. I know that I am not the ego—I am consciousness.

S: I felt the same way. Now throw away all of the techniques, theories and concepts about finding out who you are. Someone else's ideas about the ego and consciousness are of absolutely no use to you. Look for yourself. Sense it for yourself. What are you referring to when you say 'I'? <u>What are you referring to when you say 'I' am suffering; 'I' am at peace; 'I' am tired? Make this your own. Bring this to an end now! Dig in and find out for yourself, by yourself, in your own experience.</u> Reading books for another thirty years is not necessary. Get to the bottom of this now.

Q: Wow, I do feel a sense of urgency now. I'll let this simmer and let you know how it goes.

2

False Expectations

Question: Last week I mentioned to you that I felt that the understanding was really sinking in. I noticed that my life was flowing along smoothly. There was a sense that my work was 'getting done', and there was no sense that 'I' was doing it. I just did whatever work I needed to do at the moment smoothly and easily with no resentment or regrets.

This week I started a new job and things have changed. It's a completely new career for me and I'm required to commute over three hours each day. I'm doing work that I really don't enjoy, and I don't think I can last in this field for long. I lost that peaceful, flowing feeling that I enjoyed at work previously, and I'm disappointed because I feel like the understanding was really sinking in and my life was flowing along easily. Do I need to reconsider the basic understanding? I'd appreciate any direction you can offer.

Stephen: Good to hear from you again. You said, 'There was a sense that my work was 'getting done', and there was no sense that 'I' was doing it'. This is a good indication that the understanding is having its affect. You have seen through the false sense of self and seen that you are not the doer. Knowing your self as awareness and not the doer, there will be a natural sense of peacefully flowing with whatever presents itself. You know this for yourself now. What were just concepts of non-duality are now your living experience. You have a good understanding of the basics.

You mentioned that things have changed, you've started a new career doing work that you really don't enjoy and that you've lost the peaceful, flowing feeling. The fundamental understanding is that you are not the doer, and that what you are in essence is awareness. This has not changed and will never change. You may change careers, you may like or dislike your job, you may have a sense of fulfillment or disappointment, but you are always awareness. Awareness cannot be lost.

Everything can arise in you including disappointment in a new job and the frustrations that go along with that. Sometimes there can be false expectations about the effect this understanding has in our daily experience. If we expect that we'll now enjoy doing work we're not suited for, there's sure to be disappointment. Everything arises in awareness: even an unsatisfactory occupation. Is awareness affected?

3

Which is the True Mystical Experience?

Question: I've done a lot of reading and meditating, and I've had some mystical experiences through the years so I feel that I know what's being referred to when I read the words 'consciousness is all there is, and I am that'. It's really become clear on several occasions that I've had what, I suppose, could be called 'mystical' experiences.

On one occasion, while I was eating dinner, there was a direct realization, a knowing and experiencing myself as a functional aspect of the universe. 'I' was not eating, but the universe was eating itself, digesting itself and forming itself into its own body. There was no entity here called 'me' that was eating, there was just a functioning happening. Another time, while reading a book on spirituality and metaphysics, I read a line that said, 'your essential nature is consciousness and consciousness is infinite'. Upon reading those words, I had another direct realization, a knowing and experience that I had no center. There was nothing I could point to and say 'this is me'. Thoughts were happening but I wasn't thinking them. My body was moving, but I wasn't moving it. I felt I was there, somewhere, but I couldn't point anywhere in particular and say, 'here I am'. There was a sense of presence but it was not localized in my body. There wasn't the heavy sense of 'me'.

During these mystical experiences, there's a sense of peace, a lightness that's very easy and flowing. I like it! But they pass, and I find myself back with the heavy sense of ego. It's disappointing, frankly.

Stephen: So which is the mystical experience, and which is real? Is the ego real? Are 'you' digesting your food and creating your body? Are 'you' thinking the thoughts? Or is it true that, as you say, 'thoughts are happening, but I wasn't thinking them', and 'there is no entity here called 'me', just a functioning happening?' I think you know the truth of the matter, and you've seen it for yourself! You are pure awareness. You are infinite, without a center. There is no place you can point to and say, 'this is me!' You are the peaceful, flowing spaciousness. The heavy experience of the ego is the dream-like experience! What you're calling a mystical experience is a description of your natural state!

4

I Feel I May Need a Teacher

Question: My personality is such that I've never really grown attached to any particular teacher or any particular spiritual group. I do feel an affinity to the teachings of non-duality, especially Advaita and Zen. When I first started reading spiritual material I read mostly authors who had a Christian mystical background such as Joel Goldsmith's work, and *A Course in Miracles*. I felt comfortable with this because my own religious background was Christian, although I've always had an intuitive sense that all religious philosophies pointed to the same fundamental truth.

I'm now at the point where I feel that reading and thinking about this by myself may be fruitless. I feel that I may need a teacher to help clear things up for me, however, I'm generally skeptical of so called gurus and teachers, and I'm definitely not the devotional type. Is a teacher necessary for this understanding to come to fruition or can I do it on my own?

Stephen: Ultimately, what are all of the ancient traditions and teachers pointing out? Isn't it the fact that you are not a limited, separate person directing his own life; and that what you are in essence is Life Itself, Intelligence, Pure Consciousness, God, or the Buddha Mind?

You exist. You are aware. Is a teacher needed to know this? A teacher may remind you of what you *are*, and what you *are not*, and point you back to this fundamental truth time and again until you realize it for yourself, or until you get sick and tired of hearing it and you move on to another teacher who tells you the same damned thing!

When you see and know for yourself what the ancient traditions and teachers are pointing out, initially, questions and doubts may arise. You may feel the need to discuss them with a teacher. But, even then, you already know the answers. You are teaching yourself what you already know, and the understanding comes to fruition on its own.

There is no need to become attached to any teacher or spiritual group. As it's stated in Zen: No teacher! No teaching! No student!

5

There's a Screaming Contradiction

Question: Okay, so I'm seeing a clear theme in all of these talks and writings on non-duality, but there's a *screaming* contradiction! On one hand it's stated that there is 'no one here' who can do anything, and then on the other hand, 'I' (who apparently doesn't exist) am told to find out who 'I' am and to find out what is 'my' true nature. What's the deal? Is there anything I can do or not?

Stephen: Yes, there is an apparent contradiction, isn't there? I'll try to clarify. Now keep in mind that language is dual by nature as I try to communicate what the non-dual deal is. The fact is that everything is happening. 'Doing' is happening through you, through me, through everyone. There is doing, but no separate doer. There is thinking, but no separate thinker. There is action, but no separate actor. The source of all of this doing, thinking, and acting is an absolute mystery, have you noticed? Do you doubt this? Look for yourself. Are you making your heart beat or your lungs breathe? Are you making your eyes see or your ears hear? Are you controlling your own thoughts or feelings?

If there's a sense that there is a you there who can do things, a you who has control over your life, I'm asking that you do the following: find out for yourself and by yourself, what is this me that I feel I am? Who or what am I? Is there anyone or anything here that is in control? Is there a separate entity that can be found and pointed out as me? Find out for yourself, and the screaming contradiction will be clarified. If you can't find anyone there who is in control, but you stubbornly cling to the idea that you are still in control of your life, then go ahead and exercise your control. Make yourself have only happy thoughts and feelings this week. Let me know how it goes. So there is 'no one here' who can do anything, but things can be done! That's the non-dual deal!

6

Isn't This Just Another 'Doing'?

Question: I read your correspondence entitled *There's a Screaming Contradiction*, and I think I understand the fact that, as you say, 'There is doing, but no separate doer', and that, 'The source of all of this doing, thinking, and acting is an absolute mystery'. This seems to be the case and I cannot really question that. But then you go on to say, 'Find out for yourself and by yourself, what is this me that I feel I am? Who or what am I?' Isn't this just another doing? I've been reading and listening to other non-dual teachers, and they are saying that there is nothing to do, and that doing anything is merely a continuation of the problem of seeking and suffering.

Stephen: Suffering and seeking is caused by a fundamental misconception you have about who or what you are. If you believe yourself to be a separate person apart from all others and the rest of creation, you will experience a sense of alienation and loneliness. You will find yourself suffering and seeking (in various forms) to heal the separation and alienation. In your seeking you may come across someone who offers you a concept that acts as an antidote to the original misconception of being a separate person apart from the rest of creation. This contrary concept is 'You are not a separate limited person, you are in fact Life Itself, Pure Consciousness'. But you may not believe it immediately as it is contrary to what you have believed and experienced all of your life.

So you are told, 'Don't believe my words, but find out for yourself: who are you? What is your essential nature? Are you separate or are you pure consciousness?' This is using one concept to remove another. As Ramana Maharshi has put it, 'You're using one thorn as a tool to remove another thorn that is lodged painfully in your own foot. When the thorn is removed from your foot you can throw them both away as neither is necessary!'

Saying that nothing can be done to alleviate suffering in order to remain true to the concept of non-duality makes what can be a potent tool into a sterile and lifeless religious philosophy. It sounds good when read in a book, but it becomes impractical and dead. On the other hand, suggesting that we do more than question the primary misconception that 'I am a separate, limited person' is counterproductive. As you put it, 'merely a continuation of the problem of seeking and suffering', and only adds to the sense of personal doership, which is the core problem and cause of suffering.

7

Just Another Term for Enlightenment?

Question: What do you mean by 'Living in Peace: The Natural State?' (the title of your website). Is this just another phrase for enlightenment? I've attended many retreats, satsangs, and meetings of all sorts with fellow seekers, and there seems to be a lot of confusion about what enlightenment is. It seems that there is an assumption that everyone knows what it is, but it's obvious that most of us really don't. I've heard stories about how people have had awakening and enlightenment experiences, and then they feel they've lost it, or it's now deepening, or they are now embodying the awakening experience, and so on. At the same time, these folks are still suffering and are telling the same stories of personal pain and anguish.

Stephen: I use the phrase 'Living in Peace: The Natural State' because it's very simple, direct, and practical. The term 'Natural State' expresses the fact that what's being pointed out here is indeed just that: your Natural State. It's not something that's alien to you, something that you must attain; but, in fact, what you already are and always have been. I use the phrase 'Living in Peace' because it's a simple, realistic way to describe the daily experience of living in the Natural State.

The terms enlightenment and awakening, among others, have become so widely used that they have many different meanings, as you've seen in discussions with your acquaintances. There's also a sense that we are apart from these states, that we must attain them, and that only special beings are able to do so. The phrase 'Living in Peace: The Natural State' is just another set of concepts, but I feel it's the best way to describe this in simple and realistic terms.

Q: If you can, please put it in terms of what it *is* and what it *is not!*

S: What is enlightenment? Enlightenment doesn't exist. You don't exist. When this is seen there's a sense of living in peace, the natural state. Who lives in peace? I don't know, but there is peace and it is the natural state. It's really quite a mystery. Everything is as it is, right now: the good, the bad and the ugly. This is it. Nothing more. What it *is not?* It's not anything that can be described. Especially states of bliss, all-knowing wisdom, or loving-kindness: these ideas lead to false expectations.

Q: I'm not satisfied with this answer.

S: Well, then I suggest you answer these two questions in your own experience: what is awareness, and what are you? When you get to the bottom of this, you won't feel the need to attend any more retreats, satsangs or meetings, and your questions about enlightenment and awakening will be dissolved like the sugar in your morning coffee.

8

What Can I Expect to Get Out of This?

Question: If this understanding becomes, as you put it, 'my daily living experience', what can I expect to get out of this? And don't say, 'Nothing', please! I understand the non-dual approach and terminology; but if there truly is 'nothing' to get, then you're wasting your time, my time and everyone else's, no?

Stephen: <u>Believing yourself to be something you are not, and overlooking the fact of what you truly are, is the cause of psychological suffering.</u> When you believe and experience yourself to be a separate, individual person who must make your own way in the world, there's a sense of insecurity and anxiety underlying most of your daily experiences. When it is seen for yourself that your essential nature is pure awareness, and that the person you believed yourself to be is just a bundle of concepts, memories, and beliefs, the sense of personal insecurity and anxiety ceases.

Q: I do see the cause (false belief) and effect (suffering) process. There was a two-year period in my early twenties that I was experiencing terrible anxiety attacks that were brought on by pains I was having in my chest. Of course the pain in my chest added to or created more anxiety and there was a circular pattern of cause-effect-cause-effect.

Several times I had such excruciating pain in my chest that I felt I was having a heart attack: they were that debilitating! I believed I must have pre-mature heart disease. That was the only logical explanation to me at the time (I was only twenty years old). This went on for about two years, and then I couldn't take it anymore. I went to a medical doctor and there were no medical issues found, so I was referred to a psychologist. The psychologist explained how the psychosomatic process works. Believing that I had heart disease caused an occasional pain in my chest that led to more anxiety about having heart disease that led to more pain in my chest (increasingly severe and often). He recommended a couple of books about the process that I could read, too.

As soon as I understood this process, and I knew there was nothing wrong with my heart, the anxiety stopped and the chest pains stopped. After suffering with this for two years, it was gone within a week! There were a few occasions since then that I had little 'flutters' or pains in my chest, but I know there's nothing wrong; it's not uncommon. So there have been no attacks of anxiety or pain once I saw and understood the process.

S: Thank you for sharing your story! Your story illustrates exactly what you can 'get' out of this understanding. Learning that you did not have a diseased heart (confirmed by your doctor), and understanding the process of cause and effect, anxiety and physical pain, your suffering ended almost immediately. And when, as you put it, the flutters or pains in your chest recurred, you knew there was nothing wrong, and that they were common and normal so you didn't fall for the false belief. When you understand for yourself that you are not the separate person you believed yourself to be (cause), the suffering (effect) can come to an end. There may be occasions when the belief in being a separate person arises again, but you know it's not true so you don't fall for it. You are not a separate person! Your essential nature is pure consciousness!

9

Medical Doctors, Psychologists, and Psychiatrists

Question: In your correspondence entitled *What Can I Expect to Get Out of This?* The questioner mentioned that they sought the services of a medical doctor and psychologist. It seemed to be a necessity in that person's case and it worked out well. I, too, have sought and received counseling for what has been diagnosed as manic depression (bipolar disorder). Over the past thirty years I've been given prescriptions for and taken many types of medication. The counseling and medication has been helpful for me, but I'd like to be finished with it. Can these teachings do this for me?

Stephen: I suggest you stick with whatever plan that you and your doctors feel is best for you. The ideas offered here are in no way intended to replace the medical support and counseling you're currently receiving. You may find some psychologists and psychiatrists that incorporate these types of concepts into their approach. But, again, that needs to be a decision made between you and your doctor.

10

But I am a Separate Person: I am Not You!

Question: I am a separate person! No matter how many times it's stated or how much I try to convince myself, or others try to convince me, you can not deny that I am not you! This is obviously absurd! You are not aware of my thoughts and feelings. You don't have to feed my children, make my mortgage and car payments if I lose my job. I exist as a separate person: I am here and you are there! To deny this is absolute insanity! If that's not insane, what is?

Stephen: Yes, that would be absolutely insane, no doubt! I definitely don't make your mortgage or car payments, and you are responsible for feeding your children and keeping your job. In relative terms, you are there and I am here. You have your life and responsibilities, and I have mine.

The question being asked here is 'Who or what are you in essence?' We've been able to define ourselves in relative terms. Can you define yourself in absolute terms? What is it about you that never changes? What is it about you and me that's the same?

Q: It could be said that my awareness has never changed, and that both you and I have awareness: this I know. But you are not aware of the same things I am. This is obvious and undeniable!

S: Yes, we agree that the objects of awareness are relative. Is awareness relative or absolute?

Q: Well, there's my awareness and your awareness. As we agreed, you are aware of your experiences, not mine.

S: Well, we agreed that the objects of awareness are relative and different. It's the very nature of the mind to separate, classify, and judge. This cannot be denied, and to do so would be insane. Now let's get to the heart of the matter. When you say 'my awareness', who or what is this 'me' that says 'my awareness'? Does this 'me' really exist?

Q: I don't know. I can't answer that.

S: Well, you started our conversation by emphatically declaring your own existence as a separate person. And just by considering some of the basic facts you now say, 'I don't know'. Can you find out if you are truly a separate, independent person in essence? We know you exist in relative terms, but what are you in essence? What are you in absolute terms?

Q: What do you mean by 'absolute terms?'

S: By absolute terms (for the purpose of our discussion) I'm referring to that which never changes, that which cannot be denied. You cannot deny your own existence, by doing so you immediately confirm it. To say, 'I don't exist', is proof that you do. But who are you, or what are you? You know the person. But what is awareness? Does the person have awareness, or does awareness 'have' the person?

Q: I'll have to ponder this for a while!

11

The Never-Ending Nightmare

Question: After we talked last week I felt that the understanding had become my living experience. I knew myself as awareness. It was simple and obvious. Thoughts, feelings, sensations all arose in me, and did not affect my essential nature as awareness. I felt the peacefulness as the underlying foundation in all of my daily experiences. I saw that anything could arise in me and that it didn't matter what arose. I was always awareness: peaceful and free. This lasted until Wednesday morning when I woke up after having a disturbing dream in which I had a disagreement with someone from a previous relationship. I woke up somewhat agitated by this, and the mental agitation continued all day. As the day went on the mental agitation increased, and I found myself having thoughts that I had lost it, I shouldn't be annoyed and upset like this over a dream if I really had the understanding, I shouldn't be feeling this way. A sense of frustration and sadness grew as I felt like I'd never really get this and live in peace. How could a dream upset me to this degree?

I felt a disturbing energy sort of bubbling in me the entire day. There was annoyance, disappointment, sadness, and anger. I can understand having a disturbing dream at night and being upset by that. But I feel like the mental disturbance should quickly dissipate as soon as I wake up and realize it was just a dream, right?

Stephen: So you had a disturbing dream during the night, you woke up, and spent the rest of the day in another disturbing dream. Is there any difference between dreaming while asleep or dreaming while awake?

Q: Essentially they're the same. I had a nightmare while sleeping and it just kept on going even after I woke up. It's obvious to me now that the story about losing the understanding, and I'll never be at peace, and I shouldn't be feeling this way was just more (day) dreaming. And it added to the mental agitation and led to sadness and more suffering.

How can this happen? How can I get so caught up in a daydream and suffer so much because of it?

S: Well, the key is that you've now seen that dreaming happens when you're sleeping and during the day when awake. It was all a dream. Seeing the dream as a dream, you snap out of it, and the suffering stops. As you mentioned, there may be 'a disturbing energy sort of bubbling in you', but you know it's just that—a bubbling energy. Is there a problem with bubbling energy if there's no story or dream associated with it, or labeling it 'bad' and feeling that 'I should not be having this?'

Q: It's clear now. Thanks, again.

12

Emotional Detachment and Control

Question: In most of my relationships with others I feel a sense of objectivity and an ability to avoid becoming attached or overwhelmed by my emotions toward the other person. It feels like a healthy sense of objectivity, not a cold, distant, detached feeling. I love my family and friends and I have warm, emotional feelings toward them, but emotions don't overtake me. There's one exception that I have not been able to overcome and that's with my children.

Anytime there's a situation in which one of my children's happiness, health or well-being is involved, I feel overwhelmed with emotions. Sometimes there's pride, anger, sadness, fear or guilt that arises and I can't seem to control these feelings at all.

Stephen: This teaching is not about detachment from your feelings and emotions or trying to control them. You are not in control of your thoughts, feelings and emotions. There is no 'controller' there who can decide which thoughts and emotions can arise or not.

Q: Well, I'm able to control my emotions toward my friends and family, it's only with my children that I feel out of control.

S: There's a sense of healthy objectivity that arises in your relationships with your friends, and you find this acceptable, and feel you're in control. Sometimes overwhelming emotions arise when your children's happiness, health or well-being is involved, and you find this unacceptable, and you feel out of control. Do you control which emotions arise: either the acceptable or unacceptable emotions?

Q: Shouldn't I feel the same sense of emotional objectivity and detachment toward everyone, whether they're my children or not?

S: What you should or shouldn't feel is speculation, isn't it? You said that you were in control of your emotions towards your friends. Are you really? Is there a controlling entity there who can control his emotions?

Q: I can't really find an entity that is in control. I do feel very emotionally attached to my children, and I feel that I want to be able to control my emotions toward them. It bothers me that I can't get control of these emotions.

S: You say that you can't really find an entity that's in control, but you don't seem sure about it. Look for yourself. Find out if there is a controlling entity in you who can exercise control over his emotions.

This teaching is not about being detached from or controlling your emotions. It's not about what you should or shouldn't feel. This teaching is about seeing and knowing for yourself that you are not a separate, controlling entity, and that what you are in essence is pure awareness. Knowing yourself as pure consciousness all emotions are free to arise and fall in you. You may be laughing joyously one moment and crying desperately the next. Everything is as it is. There is nothing that should or shouldn't be. There's no detachment from anything because there's no one there who can detach or attach to anything. Consciousness is all there is, and you are that!

13

Show Me This Nothing

Question: What exactly is the Natural State and what is its relationship to awareness? How do I come upon or recognize the Natural

State? Will I feel different than I feel right now? Can I go in and out of it?

Stephen: It's nothing. There is no such thing. How do you define 'nothing'? Can you come upon or recognize nothing? Can you feel nothing? Can you go in and out of nothing? If you come upon and recognize nothing, it becomes something, and that's not it. If you can feel nothing, it becomes something, and that's not it. If you can go in and out of nothing, it becomes something, and that's not it.

Q: Show me this nothing.

S: Without referring to any preconceived notions you have about awareness, can you tell me anything about it?

Q: [about a minute of silence passes]

S: What can you say about awareness?

Q: Well, words kept coming up to describe it, but immediately I saw that no words applied.

S: Are you aware? What is awareness? Look again.

Q: [a few moments of silence pass] Yes, I am aware.

S: What is awareness? Is it a thing?

Q: [silence] No, it just is, but it's not a thing in the usual sense of the word.

S: Can you get away from this awareness?

Q: [silence]

S: Isn't this awareness your essential nature? Awareness is what you are, isn't it?

Q: How could I get away from awareness? Everywhere I go, there it is.

S: Yes, awareness is your essential nature. You are awareness. You can't get away from awareness: you are it. The Natural State is what you are, awareness. So your questions about the Natural State, recognizing it, going in and out of it, and how it feels: can you answer these questions now?

Q: They seem off the mark now

S: Can you recognize awareness?

Q: I am awareness. Can awareness recognize itself? That's just more thinking. Awareness is, period.

S: Yes, awareness is. Your other question: do you feel different now?

Q: Awareness is not a feeling; it just is.

S: Yes, awareness just is. It's not a feeling. Can you go in and out of awareness?

Q: [silence] I am awareness. Can awareness go in and out of awareness? That's more conceptualization. Awareness is not conceptual.

S: So awareness just is, but it is no thing.

Q: I see that now, thank you.

14

Suffering Over the Suffering of Others

Question: One thing stands out that I have a difficult time reconciling is the suffering of others. I have family members who have various medical and psychological issues. I have a parent who has health problems, siblings who are challenged by alcoholism, cancer, anxiety and depression, and their children have serious medical issues as well.

I have yet to find a way of seeing the suffering of others in a different light. How do you view it? I would like to resolve the suffering that arises here in response to the suffering that I witness.

Stephen: First, let's differentiate between pain and suffering. Pain is physical and sometimes requires medical attention, this is clear. Suffering is psychological. In an otherwise physically healthy individual, the root cause of psychological suffering is a misconception about who or what one is in essence.

If you believe yourself to be a separate, independent person, who must control his own life, there will be a sense of anxiety, loneliness, separateness, and suffering underlying your daily experiences. Believing yourself to be a separate person, you'll view others as separate, too. You'll assume they're experiencing themselves as separate and suffering the same plight as you. When it's realized that you are not a separate person, and what you are is pure awareness, the sense of separation, anxiety, loneliness, and the need to control falls away. What's left is a sense of peace and ease underlying all of your daily experiences. Knowing that there is no separate person 'here' in you who can suffer, now you know there is no separate person 'there' who can suffer. Others may be under the influence of the misconception of being a separate person, but you've seen it's not true.

You may have an urge to help others with their pain and suffering. Nisargadatta Maharaj told Bob Adamson 'the greatest help that can be given to anyone is to take them beyond the need for further help'. The first step in helping others with their psychological suffering is to be free of the need for help your self.

15

I Need to be Guided Home

Question: I had a very interesting reaction to reading your essay entitled *Reflections*. I became more and more tense and angry as you piled on question after question with seemingly provided answers. It must be that imagined 'I' that responded with those reactions. I have realized that I am that untouched field of awareness, and yet the connection with the body/mind continues. It's almost like there is a fog or something, a forgetfulness that keeps me from fully seeing the Truth without the sense of I.

I was particularly interested in the following from your essay entitled, *Reflections*: *'Seeing some 'thing' implies division, which implies naming, which implies recognizing, which implies the past, which implies time, which implies thought. Can we see without dividing, without naming, without recognizing, without the past, without time, without thought?'* Well, can we? How can I realize what you're pointing to here? I know I'm in the general vicinity, I just need to be guided home—I seem to have lost my way.

Stephen: Tension and anger arise in awareness. The imagined I arises in awareness. The source of tension, anger, and the imagined I is an absolute mystery! Reactions happen, but the imagined I cannot react at all. It is just imagination. Everything can appear in awareness. You've realized that you are the untouched field of awareness, but have you realized that *everything* can arise in you including a connection with the body/mind, a sense of I, a fog, a forgetfulness, anger, and tension?

There is no truth to see and there is no 'me' to see it. This is a fact! There is only seeing, which is awareness, which is what you always are.

You asked about the pointers in the essay *Reflections*: 'Can we see without dividing, without naming, without recognizing, without the past, without time, without thought?'—Dividing, naming, recognizing; this is a description of the thinking process. What is it that sees this process? Awareness, right? Awareness (you) witnesses the thinking process. The thinking process is just another appearance in awareness. There's no need to get rid of the dividing, naming etc., nor is there any way to get rid of it. *Everything* arises in awareness, including the thinking process. Home is awareness. You *are* home!

There was an expectation arising in you that having a sense of I, anger, tension, fog, forgetfulness, a connection with the body/mind means that you are not home and that you had lost your way. These are all false expectations, just more thoughts appearing in you. *No matter what* arises in you, you are always Home!

16

But There is Still the Appearance of 'I'

Question: I can't tell you how many times I have looked for that separate 'I' and found nothing, yet the suffering continues. I have seen that it is a false dilemma, if there is no 'I', there is nothing to do about it except see it for what it is and discard it. I will keep looking, and I appreciate your words of encouragement.

Stephen: What you're calling 'suffering' is just a bubbling, agitating energy arising in the body. 'Suffering' is assigning a 'me and my story' to the bubbling, agitating energy. You've already seen that you are awareness, and you found there is no separate 'I'. There's nothing more for you to do. The rest happens on its own (as it always has been happening).

Q: That's a relief! I was just sitting and going over it in this way: there is awareness, which is free and clear, and there is thinking on top of that. As I sat in a chair, seen from the perspective of an apparent 'other', I could be relaxing, or I could be deep in thought worrying about problems, or planning a vacation. But seen from the perspective of Awareness, without buying into thought, there is a sunny day, a light breeze, the sounds of children playing, and the smell of barbecue. I have to admit, though, there is still sometimes the appearance of being an individual—especially when I'm around and conversing with people. I trust that everything will take care of itself.

S: There is no separate, controlling entity in you. But, there is a person or body/mind there. The person has certain characteristics of its own: physical appearance, likes and dislikes, tendencies, and other personal traits. When the person comes in contact and converses with others, the sense of 'I' can arise during the interaction. This is part of the play of consciousness, and is not a problem.

Your essential nature is pure awareness. The person arises and falls in you. The person is not a controlling entity, it is merely another expression of consciousness, and there is no need or way to discard the person, or the sense of 'I' that arises with it. Seeing and knowing yourself as awareness, not a separate controlling entity, you are freedom itself. The person and the sense of 'I' are free to arise and fall in you.

17

Liberation From the Mind

Question: It's been about a month since we last spoke. I don't have any more questions. After years of reading and struggling to understand, I'm finding that I have no interest in reading, going to meetings, retreats or any of it. When questions do arise, I see they are meaningless, and they just fall away. What's left is awareness, peaceful and free.

Stephen: Yes, it's amazing how quickly the questions fall away when you see that the questions, the reading, and struggling were disturbing the peace that was already there. What you were seeking was the peaceful easiness of your natural state of awareness, and that, you never lost.

Q: The same old stories, doubts, and worries have come up on occasion, but they have lost their power. Nothing can trouble me but my own imagination. It's so obvious now.

S: Seeing the truth that nothing can trouble you but your own imagination, renders the stories, doubts, and worries powerless. This is liberation from the mind. And as you say, what's left is awareness: peaceful and free!

Q: The simplicity of this is mind-boggling. I've read for years about how simple this is, and now I see it for myself.

S: Enjoy!

18

Egoic Interactions and Confrontations

Question: What effect does this understanding have on one's relationships? Isn't it difficult to relate to someone who is caught up in the ego when you are free of that?

Stephen: It's much more difficult for two egos to relate. The egoic experience is one of insecurity, lack, and fear. Believing yourself to be an individual ego, your relationships are fundamentally insecure, lacking and fearful. Knowing yourself as pure awareness and not a separate ego, your relationship with everyone and everything changes.

Q: But isn't it frustrating to interact with others who are completely caught up in their ego? Don't you feel like you're being pulled into egoic interactions and confrontations?

S: This realization reveals the fact that everything is happening, and that there is no one who is doing anything. Even the ego, which is the personal sense of doer-ship, is just happening. Does the ego create the ego? Seeing that there is no one in control here in me, it is also seen that there is no one in control in the other. Who is confronting whom? All interactions and confrontations are the Source interacting with and confronting itself.

Along with this is a sense of acceptance of whatever is happening. There is no one here accepting things, but there is a sense of acceptance. Confrontational interactions arise and fall: awareness remains pure, peaceful, and unaffected.

19

Love and Intimate Relationships

Question: I've heard and read that our natural state of awareness can also be called love. Can you expand upon this?

Stephen: The presence of awareness with the absence of 'me' is love.

Q: Is the absence of me required for there to be love? Can't love be experienced in personal, intimate relationships?

S: Love is the essence of all existence. Love is the natural state of all being. All there is, is love. Without love, nothing is. Love is not personal. There is no 'my' love or 'your' love: there is just love.

Q: How is love experienced on a personal level in intimate relationships? Surely, there must be a 'you' and a 'me' to know and experience love!

S: When two are involved in a personal relationship there are times when the sense of 'you' and 'me' (ego) falls away in each person. In the absence of the sense of 'you' and 'me' there is love. This is the sense of peace, joy, and blissful oneness for which we're all longing: it's our natural state. When the sense of ego arises again, the natural state of love is personalized by the mind and claimed as a personal experience of the ego. The two egos then assume that the other is the source of their love. This, of course, leads to fear of loss, jealousy and a host of other painful emotions.

Q: That makes sense, but I don't 'love' everyone. There is a special sense of love I have for my partner. Aren't there different types of love?

S: On a personal level, there are different types of relationships, and there can be a special attraction between partners based on biological and psychological compatibility. But there are not different types of love or a special love. Love is the essence of all being; it's absolute, unconditional, and impersonal.

Q: How will this recognition help me with my personal relationships?

S: Knowing yourself as pure awareness and not a separate ego, there is the recognition that your essential nature is love. You are what you have always been seeking. You don't need anyone or anything to fill the sense of emptiness, loneliness, and separation that is the egoic experience. The fear of loss, jealousy, and other painful emotions that are the essence of egoic relationships fall away. You are able to truly enjoy the beauty of all human relationships in complete freedom, love, and peace. Love is your natural state.

20

I Feel Absolutely Worthless

Question: There are times when I feel absolutely worthless. I've been unemployed for several months due to an economic slow down in my trade. I've been searching for a new job, but nothing has panned out yet. My family's needs are being met, so I'm not under any severe pressure to provide for them financially at this point. But sometimes I am overwhelmed by a sense of worthlessness. My self-worth seems completely tied to my function as a provider for my family.

Stephen: Have you noticed that in absolute terms everything is worthless, meaningless, and without purpose? What a blow to the ego! Value or worthlessness only has meaning in relative terms and on a personal basis. Who is worthless or valuable to whom? On a personal basis you may be the best provider, parent, spouse, friend, sibling, child, or employee one day, and the next day you may be considered the worst. When your sense of self is based on the person with it's functions and attributes, you will experience swings in your sense of self-worth. But are you a person?

Q: My family considers me to be a person and their provider!

S: Your family considers you to be a provider; your parents, a child; your buddies, a friend; your employer, an employee. But what do you consider yourself to be? If you believe what others say you are, then your self-worth is subject to their valuations and judgments, and you'll suffer accordingly. Your essential nature is consciousness, not the person.

Q: That sounds all well and dandy, but it doesn't help with my sense of worthlessness.

S: A sense of worthlessness can only arise for a person and in relation to others. But are you a person? Are you the provider, the friend, or the employee? If you want to resolve your sense of worthlessness, look into this for yourself. The sense of worthlessness you are experiencing may be the motivating factor that leads to liberation from all that you are not. You are beyond the person and its sense of value or worthlessness. You are not the provider, the friend or the employee. Who are you?

21

Permanent States?

Question: I've recently noticed that whatever state I'm experiencing at the time, I feel like I will always be in that state. Sometimes I feel peaceful, relaxed, and at ease, and I'll think, 'Ahhh, finally I've made it! My life has worked out perfectly. I am at peace forever!' And then a day or two passes and my circumstances change. I'll feel tired and frustrated, and I'll think, 'I'm doomed! My life will never work out the way I want it to. I'll be miserable and depressed forever!' And this, too, passes. At the time, I actually believe and feel that I will always be in the state I'm experiencing. This fluctuation is disappointing. What's happening here?

Stephen: All states are temporary. States of happiness and sadness are mental states, and they come and go in awareness. If you expect or believe that any state will last forever, you'll be disappointed. What's happening is that you are identifying with states of mind rather than your true nature. Your true nature is consciousness and is always here witnessing the states that arise and fall.

Q: What can I do about this tendency to identify with states of mind?

S: You said, 'At the time, I actually believe and feel that I will always be in the state I'm experiencing'. This shows that, in retrospect, you know the states of happiness and sadness are temporary. Any state, feeling, or thought that can be identified and labeled as happy, sad or anything else for that matter, is just a mental state, and is not your true nature. As soon as the thought arises that 'I am happy' or 'I am sad', know that it cannot be you.

You are that which is aware of all states. 'I am' is the only truth that can be spoken. 'I am happy' or 'I am sad' is not true.

22

I Disagree With Everything You're Saying

Question: I don't understand most of what you're saying, and the parts that I do understand, I completely disagree with you.

Stephen: What I'm talking about is so fundamental and basic that it cannot be understood. It's too simple to be understood. How can you 'understand' consciousness? We can try to understand concepts, but concepts about consciousness are not consciousness. Anything that we can agree or disagree about is irrelevant, but can you disagree that you exist, you are aware?

Q: But you said that consciousness is all there is, and I am That. You're implying that nothing is real except consciousness. And you've quoted Nisargadatta's words that nothing can trouble you but your own imagination. This implies that my problems are not real and are just imaginary. How can you say what is real or unreal, which problems are real or imaginary. Then, if I disagree with you, you say it's irrelevant!

S: Let's keep this practical. What do you want to get out of this? Surely you want more than understanding concepts, and agreeing or disagreeing about what is real or imaginary?

Q: Ultimately, I'm interested in happiness, joy, and peace. I'm frustrated by what seem to be inconsistent, contradictory concepts. My life seems to be like a pendulum that swings from happiness to sadness constantly. I'd like to be free of my suffering like this.

S: So you're interested in happiness, joy, and peace themselves: not the concepts of happiness, joy, and peace.

Q: Yes, of course.

S: Sitting here right now we can hear the wind blowing through the trees, we feel the cool breeze on our faces, we see the birds in the trees and we hear them chirping. We feel the chairs we're sitting in, we see the clouds floating by in the blue sky, and we feel the sun's heat on our backs. We smell the barbecue cooking on the grill. Do we have any problems right now?

Q: No, but if someone approached us here and attacked us with a bat, we'd have a problem. We couldn't survive if there wasn't a sense of concern about our safety and well-being in the future. I have to think about my education, my career, my family, my finances, etc.

S: So sitting here right now we have no problems and no suffering. There is a sense of peace and happiness as we are aware of our surroundings. When do the problems and the suffering start?

Q: When I start thinking about the future and my responsibilities, and whether I'll be able to meet them.

S: So problems and suffering start when you're thinking about the future. Maybe things will work out as you hope, maybe they won't; you can only speculate. This thinking and speculating I'm calling imagination. Right now you know that you exist, that there is consciousness. This cannot be denied. This consciousness I'm calling real.

Consciousness, your essential nature, is always present here and now. It is the non-conceptual awareness of being. It is too fundamental and simple to 'understand', agree or disagree with. This sense of presence-awareness is the peaceful happiness you're seeking. Not the concepts of peace and happiness, but peace and happiness itself.

If you believe that your thoughts and speculations are real, your experience will seem to be like a pendulum swinging from happiness to sadness, and you'll suffer. When you see that your thoughts and speculations are imaginary, they lose their power to influence your experience. You'll notice that the pendulum swings less frequently and less drastically.

You can agree or disagree with all of these concepts. But the fact of your own being, your own existence as consciousness, cannot be denied. It's always here and now, untouched, peaceful and aware. Drop all your concepts, and enjoy the simple presence of your own being.

23

How Do I See This for Myself?

Question: I am tormented by my thoughts. There is always a drama playing in my mind. It's usually some story of conflict between me and someone else. It's my boss, a co-worker, my partner, a friend, a family member—always someone or something. It's bothersome to me because, as these dramas play out it my mind, my body suffers: my stomach churns, my neck muscles tighten, and I get headaches.

Stephen: How often have the tormenting stories of drama and conflict come true?

Q: Never. Not even once. I know this, but there are still stories playing in my mind that cause disturbing physical symptoms. I may be driving in my car, or sitting alone at home, and a story will start playing in my mind. It may go on for just a few minutes or longer at times. But, the stories usually gather momentum and then I'll start feeling physical symptoms. Once I start feeling the physical symptoms, it strikes me that I'm dreaming up this crazy story, and I'll relax a bit. But the stories just start again later.

S: So the disturbing stories have never come to pass, and you know they're just stories playing in the mind.

Q: Yes, I know they're just my imagination, but they're still happening and my body suffers from them.

S: If you're still suffering from them, there must be some part of the story that you believe to be true and real. Who is the central character or star of your stories?

Q: Me, of course.

S: Yes, of course, and you believe the star of the stories is real. And what if all the stories involving your relationships with your boss, co-workers, friends etc worked out perfectly for you? What would you get out of it, or what do you want ultimately?

Q: I want the same thing everyone else wants: happiness, peace, joy, and love.

S: The root cause of the suffering you're experiencing is the belief that you are a separate controlling entity (ego) who must guide and control his life so that his story will work out as planned and he will experience happiness, peace and joy. This is the core mistake, the essential misconception. The fact is you are not in control. There is no one or no thing there in you who is in control. There is no controlling entity who can manipulate his story so things work out as planned. What you are is pure consciousness, which is the happiness, peace and joy that you are trying to get by controlling your life story.

Q: How do I see this for myself? I've read all the books, but I haven't been able to see this for myself.

S: If you look for the ego, the 'me', you'll find it's not there. It was just an unexamined assumption. This search must be your own though! If you're searching for someone else's concept of the ego, or the 'me', you may not see this for yourself. What do *you* think of, feel, or sense yourself to be? Do you sense yourself to be the controller of your life? Do you sense yourself to be the thinker or guide of your life? What do *you* sense yourself to be?

And then look for yourself and see if you can find the thinker, the controller, the guide, the ego; whatever you feel yourself to be. If you can't find any controller, thinker or ego there, but you still feel a sense of being the ego, thinker or controller, then try to exercise that assumed control. Try to control your thoughts, your feelings, and your life story: you can't do it! When you look for yourself and see that there is no 'me' there, no thinker, no controller, no ego; the next question is, 'Then what am I?' What you are is consciousness. You are witnessing the stories and the star of all the dramas that were playing in the mind and disturbing your body.

Q: Help me see this.

S: You must look and see this for yourself! You can be told that you are not the ego, and what you are is pure consciousness. But you must see this for yourself or it's just a bunch of concepts!

24

Make This Observation

Question: I first caught wind of you after reading your poem entitled *When I Am Born* that struck me as exceptionally clear. A visit to your web site stirred up more interest. I was particularly struck by the similarity of your struggle to mine about how to live by what is inspiring in Nisargadatta's *I Am That* beyond just an intellectual understanding. I'd say I'm in a lot of turmoil about just this, and I can see no way out of it. In the four or five years my thinking has been turned upside down by Nisargadatta's brand of non-dualism, I have not found one living soul I could resonate with about this.

Stephen: Yes, it can be quite frustrating when we read Nisargadatta and seem to have a strong intellectual understanding, but our suffering continues. I found it helpful to meet and correspond with John Wheeler, and he helped me see how simple this really is. I am happy to share my experience about this with you. You will find that I have nothing new to offer you. I don't know anything that you don't already know. And you don't need anything that you don't already have. This is a fact.

The turmoil that you're experiencing, as you know, is just mental noise, stories, and dramas playing out. And, of course, you are the star and central character of all the drama. John helped me see these three facts: The turmoil just doesn't matter. There is no one here who can control the turmoil. Consciousness is all there is, and I am this consciousness.

Q: Your statement, 'There is no one here who can control the turmoil', what do you mean? Is there nothing to be done? It seems to me that even Nisargadatta exhorted earnestness and vigilant investigation. Isn't there something to be said for vigilance.

S: Yes, earnestness and vigilant investigation can be the critical factors that bring one to the recognition that there is no one here who can control the turmoil, no one here who can be vigilant, no one here who can investigate. The earnestness and vigilant investigation can reveal the fact that things are being done, but no one is doing them.

It's easy to see and feel that your heart is beating, but you are not beating your heart. It's easy to realize that your eyes are seeing, your ears are hearing, your lungs are breathing, and you are not doing any of it. But for some reason, for those of us who have suffered, there is the sense that we are in control of our thoughts, feelings, and actions. And that in order to be happy and at peace we must exercise this control.

This attempt to exercise control is the very suffering we're trying to overcome! When the suffering becomes too much to handle, the earnestness and vigilant investigation will arise in response to the suffering. And the advice of someone like Nisargadatta or Ramana to 'find out who you are' will be heeded. So this investigation will be done, and it will be seen that there is no controlling entity here, no ego, no doer. All that can be known for certain is that there is consciousness, and consciousness is what I am.

Q: I have another question for you that I can barely contain: does the terror of being the only thing that is mean anything to you?

S: As you're seeing and reading these words right now, notice the 'seeing' or the consciousness of the words. Without the seeing, without the consciousness, nothing is. Stop again for a moment. Now, notice just the seeing. There is seeing, consciousness right now, right? This consciousness is the only thing that is. You are consciousness. You are the only thing that is. Where's the terror in that? <u>The cause of terror is imagination.</u>

Q: The ebb and flow (inconsistency) of insight is currently a source of suffering.

S: The fundamental, experiential insight is that your essential nature is consciousness, not the ego (controller). Again, make this observation: sitting by yourself, watch as your attention falls on an object in your vision: a chair, a picture, a shoe, any object will do. Notice the 'seeing'. Notice the awareness of the seeing. This awareness is what you are. Without this awareness nothing else exists. When you feel that you have lost the insight, or you feel there's an ebb and flow, an inconsistency; stop and make the observation. Consciousness, you, are always there witnessing everything, including the thoughts 'I lost the insight, I'm suffering' etc.

Q: How am I to accept that I am 'the only thing that is' when I have no knowledge of being the creator, or source of the world, all who populate it, nor my own body and mind?

S: Who or what created the creator? What is the source of the source of the world? Who created the creator of your mind and body? Ultimately, *all* questions lead to one answer: I don't know! *Everything* is an absolute mystery. Have you noticed?

The only statement that can be made without doubt is 'I am'. What I am, who I am, where did I come from, where am I going—it's all a mystery.

Q: Nor am I, who am all, able to leave the confines of my body and enter anyplace or anyone else. If I am what is everything, I do not appear to be able to freely inhabit any part of 'all that I am'.

S: These are interesting abilities and skills that some people seem to exhibit. Others are able to run a four-minute mile. I'm able to do neither. These abilities and skills are interesting, but obviously not necessary to live in peace.

Q: Okay, okay! I just re-read your response and I see what you are getting at. You are making clear that I am not anything I can sense in any way. You are simply stating that I am nothing but consciousness, no more no less. Well, this leaves me with an immediate question: what about appetite, often felt as desire? Is appetite like other things you mentioned, also outside of consciousness?

S: Appetites and desires happen. The eyes are seeing, the ears are hearing; desires, appetites, feelings and thoughts are arising. What is their source? What is the source of their source? Are you the source of your thoughts, desires and appetites? It's all a mystery, isn't it?

Q: If it is not for me to control, do I just fearlessly let uncensored desire govern the actions of my body?

S: Are you in control? Who's in control of you? Do you just fearlessly let uncensored desire govern the actions of your body? Who lets you let uncensored desire govern the actions of your body? It's all a mystery, and it's all conceptual jibber-jabber. It can be interesting and entertaining to ponder these questions, but they have no relevance to what we want ultimately: peace, happiness, and joy.

The only statement that can be made without doubt is 'I am'. Knowing and experiencing yourself as 'I am' is the peace, happiness, and joy that you're seeking by exercising your intellect with all of these interesting questions. Exercising the intellect is entertaining, but it's not the source of peace. Consciousness, I AM, is always here and now. You can't get away from it: you are it.

25

Ramana Maharshi Said

Question: Ramana Maharshi said, 'That which is not present in deep dreamless sleep is not real'. The notion comes to mind that every night, dreamless sleep reveals this obvious, unchanging, self-evident Reality, which is equally present during the waking hours of typical mental chatter, though perhaps up-staged by that mental chatter and unnoticed. My question is, what can be said about what is present in dreamless sleep?

Stephen: Awareness is present with all states: the dream state, the dreamless sleep state, and the waking state. There is just one consciousness, but we can use two terms to describe it. I use 'awareness' to mean objectless consciousness. Meaning there is no subject-object relationship, there is just absolute awareness. Relative awareness is called consciousness. Consciousness arises when the subject-object relationship arises as I or I am; I am Stephen; I am happy; I am sad; I am separate, etc.

So, to your question, what can be said about what is present in dreamless sleep? It can be said that 'awareness is', period. Nothing else. You can see this for yourself when you (consciousness) wake up in the morning. The first thought of the day may be something like this, 'I have to get up for work'. What was there before this first thought? Awareness is there, without the subject-object relationship, without the 'I'. Awareness is there to see this first thought, the 'I' thought.

Q: And how is 'what is present in dreamless sleep' ever noticed during the waking hours?

S: Awareness is not an object that can be noticed. Consciousness is noticed as the sense 'I am'. So, of what practical use is any of this? You quoted Ramana's statement, 'That which is not present in deep dreamless sleep is not real'. Well, absolute awareness is present in the dreamless state, period. There is no me, no you, no world and no problems. As soon as the 'I' thought arises, the world and my problems arise: all imagination, all unreal. What you are in absolute terms is Awareness. In relative terms, all you know for sure is that you are conscious, you exist, I am. Everything else is debatable, imaginary, speculative, and conceptual.

Knowing that, as you put it, the 'typical mental chatter' is just imaginary, conceptual, and unreal, the mental chatter loses its power to influence your experience. Knowing yourself as awareness, consciousness, not the separate, fearful little me, there is a sense of peace underlying all of your daily experiences.

26

Mental Chatter and Flailing About

Question: As Bob Adamson and John Wheeler have said, the answer is not in the mind, period. Full stop. So I can stop looking there, and be still. There shouldn't be any trick to being still. But the mind remains to play a role in serving up being still, which is therefore not really stillness. I don't know what to ask anymore. Any questions are seen to be just more garb draped around this I-thought, just more posturing or defining who I am by the clever questions I claim to be mine. It's all nonsense, to the core. It's all imagination. But for some reason, or for no reason, it's difficult to let go and fall back into stillness, into the immutable silent witness that is here all along, patiently waiting out all this imaginary flailing about. Even though we all do it every night.

Stephen: The good news is there is no need to be still, no need to patiently wait out the imaginary flailing about, no need to fall back into the immutable silent witness. The mental chattering and flailing about may continue forever. There are common misconceptions that this realization requires a silent mind, or will bring on a silent mind. This is not the case. It is the nature of the mind to flail about and chatter. So what? *Everything* is free to arise and fall in you, awareness, including mental chatter and imaginary flailing about. You are the immutable silent witness, always here and now.

27

Everything Else is Irrelevant

Question: For lack of a better way to say this: I suspect that my problem is that I still identify with this body-mind. I read and believe that I am pure awareness itself, formless and unattached, in which the body, and time and space itself are but an appearance. I read the words that I am not this body-mind that I take myself to be, but rather I am the pure light of awareness that illumines consciousness and its infinite content. The words ring true, and I believe them. But then I forget. Maybe it's because I don't really understand.

Stephen: To understand, or to see clearly what awareness is and that you are awareness, make this simple observation. Sit alone quietly and watch as your attention settles on some object in the room: a chair, a table, a candle, a picture—any object will do. As your attention settles on the object, notice that there is consciousness of the object. There is a 'seeing' of the object. Notice the seeing. Now, whose 'seeing' is it? Is it your seeing? Or is it just seeing? There is consciousness of the object, but it is not your consciousness. Consciousness is not personal. It is your essential nature; it's my essential nature. Now, do you see this clearly? As you said, it is not an understanding of the mind. It is a simple recognition that you are the seeing; you are consciousness.

Q: The seeing just is. And I am that. I don't *have* that—I *am* that. I don't see the seeing. It is no thing to be seen. But there is seeing, nevertheless, no doubt. It can be seen that the seeing is what I am, my essential nature, my innermost being. But what it is, can't be said, I don't think. I can't see what it is. But I can see that it is, and that it is what I am.

S: This seeing or consciousness is what you are. Without consciousness, nothing is. This is the fundamental truth that the ancient traditions are pointing to: I AM THAT I AM. This I Am-ness is you, consciousness.

Q: That is what I recognize sometimes. Other times I feel like it is this body that has that seeing, and there could be no seeing without this body-mind apparatus. The body can be seen as an appearance in awareness, but it doesn't follow that the awareness cannot, therefore, be coming from that body-mind, or be a property of that body-mind.

Sometimes I look in the mirror and think to myself: how can you say that this body is not me, this body is not who I am? Who is saying that? How is 'whoever' saying that? How are those thoughts formed, and how are they uttered? At times like that, to make the assertion 'that is not who I am' seems like insanity, an insanity that may happen to feel good somehow.

S: The fact that you are, or I am, cannot be denied or debated. As soon as you begin to assert 'I am not' you have proved you are, I am. Anything that follows I am, can be debated or denied:

I am confused—I am clear.
I am the body—I am not the body.
I am the mind—I am not the mind.
I am Stephen—I am not Stephen.
The body is a property of awareness—awareness is a property of the body.

These are all thoughts that arise in consciousness, and all of them can be debated ad nauseum. What cannot be debated is that consciousness is, or I am.

Q: As a matter of trust in your confident tone, and the whiff of truth about it all, I can suspend judgment to at least doubt that I really am this body, and investigate as guided.

S: Do you need to suspend judgment or rely on trust to know that you exist, you are aware? Before there can be trust or suspended judgment, consciousness (you) must be there to witness it. Anything that requires trust or debate is not worth trusting or debating. No trust is required to know that consciousness is 'I am'.

Again, you said: 'The seeing just is. And I am that. I don't have that, I am that. I don't see the seeing. It is no thing to be seen. But there is seeing, nevertheless, no doubt. It can be seen that the seeing is what I am, my essential nature, my innermost being. But what it is can't be spoken, I don't think. I can't see what it is. But I can see that it is, and that it is what I am'.

Stay with that! Everything else is irrelevant.

28

Meeting with a Teacher

Question: I was reading your website *Living In Peace: The Natural State* the other day, and there is much resonance with the following that you have written on your bio page:

'After years of reading and re-reading the book, I AM THAT, I felt I had a strong intellectual understanding of the truth that Nisargadatta was pointing to, but it was not my living experience. This led to a sense of terrible frustration. I felt I needed to find someone who was living this truth and was able to help me make it my daily, living experience.

In 2004 I learned of a man called 'Sailor' Bob Adamson from Australia who was a student of Nisargadatta Maharaj and who has been helping others come to the understanding for over twenty-nine years. Bob led me to his student, John Wheeler, from Santa Cruz, California, who was also teaching in the same tradition. I met John Wheeler in 2004. Through this meeting and our conversations that followed, the intellectual understanding has become my living experience. After more than twenty years of struggling and searching for Peace, the seeking has come to an end. I am thankful to Nisargadatta Maharaj, 'Sailor' Bob Adamson, and John Wheeler who pointed me to the Peace that I already was and always have been'.

Although I've read all of Nisargardatta's work, and listened to many CDs and DVDs by many teachers, I would say that this same sense of frustration is often experienced in my daily living. What was the difference in the face-to-face meetings with John Wheeler that does not seem so apparent otherwise?

Stephen: It's like reading all the great books about how to play golf, and watching the videos on how to develop the perfect swing. Then you get your own set of clubs and head to the course. You put into practice all the great tips you learned from the books and videos. Sometimes you hit the ball right down the middle of the fairway, and other times you slice it out of bounds.

So, a sense of frustration develops. 'I've read all the books, and I have the intellectual understanding, but I'm still hitting the ball out of bounds! This is frustrating! Maybe someone can help me with my swing'. And then you meet Tiger Woods: 'Hey, Tiger, can you spend a little time helping me with my swing?' You spend a few hours with him, and he helps you see things that you already knew from your studies, but just needed clarifying and a little polishing up. So Tiger helped make the intellectual understanding become your experience on the course. Being on the spiritual path for many years we can learn a great deal. At some point frustration may develop with being on the path. We feel that we've read all that we can read, but we're still suffering. This is when meeting with someone who can help clarify things for us can be beneficial. The intellectual understanding can become your daily living experience.

What you've read and heard in all the books, CDs, and DVDs is that your essential nature is awareness: you are not the thoughts, feelings, perceptions, and beliefs that arise in you. But, for some reason, you're still identifying with the activities of the mind and suffering because of it. When the chatter and dramas of the mind are seen as unimportant, they become merely background noise. It's like having a soap opera playing on your television. You may watch the drama and enjoy it, or you may just hear it as background noise as you go about your daily business, unaffected.

A teacher will keep reminding you of this until your obsession and identification with the activities of the mind are seen through and fall away, and along with them the suffering. Ultimately, you see that you need nothing at all to be at peace. You lose interest in teachers, teachings, and being a student. You see that your search for enlightenment was an absolute joke!

29

Frustration and a Yearning to Know

Question: For the past three years I've been an avid reader of non-duality: Nisargadatta's *I Am That*, Ramana Maharshi, and many other teachers as well. There seems to have been a progression of sorts, but now the most accurate way to describe my experience is to paraphrase your words, 'there's an intellectual understanding, but it's not my daily living experience', i.e. I'm not living it! As you say, the frustration is there plus a yearning to know and be that—especially when I read about boundless peace, absolute freedom etc. What now? Any help will be gratefully accepted.

Stephen: I am happy to share everything I can with you based on my experience. You said: 'As you say, the frustration is there plus a yearning to know and be that—especially when I read about boundless peace, absolute freedom etc'. This boundless peace is at peace with the frustration and the yearning to know! The frustration and the yearning to know are absolutely free to arise in this absolute freedom!

You are awareness. Notice the awareness of these words. You are aware, yes? This awareness is what you are. Without you, nothing exists. You have been aware of frustration and a yearning to know. Are you the awareness, or the frustration and the yearning to know? Everything that arises in you will come and go. Awareness, you, are always here and now. This awareness is the absolute freedom, the boundless peace. *Everything* is free to arise and fall in you, including frustration and a yearning to know.

By the way, the frustration and the yearning to know dissolve when you see that there is nothing to know, and no way to avoid your current experience of frustration.

30

Questions, Questions Everywhere, But Not a Drop of Peace

Question: This state of pure awareness sounds like it is ignorant or ever unknowing of the mystery of life, right?

Stephen: Everything is a mystery, is it not? All I know for certain is that I exist, I am, consciousness is.

Q: Some awake ones say there is reincarnation; some say no, and some say I don't know. If you're all the same being, why are the answers different?

S: Who or what reincarnates?

Q: You now know yourself to be that, and that created this dream. So how did you come up with the idea of humans, fish, birds etc?

S: Who created all of creation? Who created the creator? This is a mystery, too.

Q: You're free now but you are still in this body (or this body is in you), and this body is going to break down, get diseased, feel pain and die. How free is that?

S: The body is not free. Freedom is *from* the body and mind, not *of* them.

Q: If everything that's happening is perfect, then if I go out and start killing people, that's perfect, too? There's no one here so nothing matters, right?

S: What is perfection? Is there any such thing? Nothing matters to whom?

Q: After you wake up the ego/mind keeps doing its thing. It's just seen to be not your real identity. If a person was on anti-depressants before, will he need them after? Depression would end, wouldn't it?

S: I'm not an M.D. or a Psychiatrist, so I follow their advice regarding therapy and medication. All of these questions and answers arise in awareness. Awareness is always here and now. These questions and answers do not affect awareness. Your essential nature is awareness. Without awareness there would be no questions or answers. Awareness must be here to witness them. It is the nature of the mind to ask questions and search for answers.

You are neither the mind nor its questions. You are awareness, that which is aware of the body and mind. Awareness is peaceful and free of the body and mind. The peaceful freedom you are seeking is your natural state. Asking questions and receiving answers will not bring you anything you don't already have, as you already are awareness—peaceful and free.

31

How Do I Get Off the Merry-Go-Round?

Question: Hi, Stephen.

You wrote: *'Awareness, you, are always here and now. This awareness is the absolute freedom, the boundless peace. Everything is free to arise and fall in you, including frustration and a yearning to know'*. What happens to me is that I notice the awareness, but then I keep getting lost in the thought-stories. How do you get off the merry-go-round?

Stephen: We love watching movies at the theater and on television. We love laughing and crying at the comedies and dramas, and getting lost in the stories. And we enjoy riding on the merry-go-round of emotion they elicit.

Think about your favorite movie and your favorite character in that movie. As you're watching the movie, you're able to enjoy the experience of the central character. You experience the drama, the emotional swings, the successes and failures of the star. You laugh, you cry, you watch in suspense as the drama unfolds. You love it all—the highs, the lows, the pleasure and the pain. You're able to get lost in the story and enjoy it because you know you are the watcher of the story, the witness of the unfolding drama. You watch the central character act out his part and you go along for the ride. You do not suffer as the story plays out, because you know you are the watcher, not the star of the movie.

The thought-stories, mental dramas, and the merry-go-round of emotions they evoke are not, by themselves, problematic, and do not cause suffering. If the stories playing out in your mind are causing you to suffer, there must be a belief in the reality and substance of the central character and star of the stories, Terry. There is a character in your life called Terry, no doubt, but she and her stories are not a problem.

You are the witness of Terry and her stories. You are the watcher, the awareness of Terry and her stories. More accurately, you are the watching, the witnessing of all the stories that come and go. How do you get off the merry-go-round? The key is to see clearly for yourself that what you are in essence is that which is watching Terry and her story unfold. You are not Terry. You are awareness. Can Terry and her story exist without you, awareness, being there to witness her? Trying to control Terry, and trying to manipulate her story so that she'll be happy and at peace is the very cause of the suffering you're trying to avoid!

You are not the author of Terry's story. Terry's story is not a problem: the good, the bad, the pleasure and the pain—none of it is problematic. If you find yourself suffering from the story, just notice the awareness, notice yourself as consciousness. The stories may continue playing in your mind, but eventually they become like background noise and have no affect on your experience.

When you know yourself as pure awareness, the stories and the merry-go-round of emotion do not cause suffering. In fact, they're a great source of entertainment and enjoyment. The happiness, the sadness, the pleasure and the pain: all are welcomed as you watch the most exciting movie ever made—your own life story.

32

Why is It So Difficult to Wake Up?

Question: Why is it so difficult to wake up? I'm interested in exactly what this natural state entails.

Stephen: Awareness is what you are. Awareness is your natural state. Do you see these words now? Are you aware of seeing these words right now? Is awareness difficult? You are this awareness. Waking up is simply the recognition that you are awareness, and that Jim and his life story is a dream.

It's the thinking, questioning, and struggling for answers that's difficult. These are all just functions of the mind, and the mind is not the source of peace. This is much easier than you could possibly imagine. If you're finding it difficult, then you're paying attention to thoughts, ideas, feelings (mind stuff), and not the simplicity of your own being—the peace that is your natural state, your essence as awareness.

33

Is There a Natural Progression?

Question: Should there be a feeling of freedom or ease?

Stephen: A feeling of freedom and ease will arise, and then a feeling of contraction and uneasiness will arise. Happy thoughts and feelings will arise, and then sad thoughts and feelings will arise. Pleasurable bodily sensations will arise, and then painful bodily sensations will arise. There is no problem with thoughts, feelings, or sensations that arise. Thoughts, feelings, and sensations are not the cause of suffering. Suffering begins when *rejection* of a thought, feeling, or sensation arises, and the sense that 'I' must take action to avoid this experience now, and in the future. And suffering begins when *acceptance* of a thought, feeling, or sensation arises, and the sense that 'I' must take action to grasp onto this experience now, and in the future.

The root cause of suffering is the belief or sense that at your core is a controlling entity, an ego, a me that can exercise control over thoughts, feelings, and sensations that arise. And that in order to be happy and at peace, 'I' must exercise this control. I must take action to ensure that I will always be happy and never be sad.

This attempt to control our thoughts, feelings, and sensations leads us down many paths throughout our lifetime. When we learn of the possibility of enlightenment, this becomes the ultimate way to achieve and maintain control over our experience. Attaining enlightenment, we assume, will give us the ultimate control over our thoughts, feelings, and sensations. <u>Enlightenment, as it turns out, is the realization that there is no one here who can become enlightened, there's no controlling entity, no ego, no separate me who can exercise control over thoughts, feelings, and sensations that arise. When this realization happens, we could say there is a surrendering to whatever arises. The recognition is that there is no one here to reject or accept what arises— there is only awareness, and awareness is what I am.</u>

So, yes, there is a constant, underlying sense of freedom and ease. This underlying sense of freedom and ease is untouched, even by feelings of contraction and uneasiness. But, you say, isn't that a contradiction? When you are at peace with war, you are always at peace—even in the midst of war! <u>When the realization dawns that there is no controlling entity there in you, there is no ego, no me in control; there is no one there to fight anymore! There's no one there to reject or accept whatever arises. All there is, is consciousness, and you are that. Therein lies the peace that surpasses all understanding.</u>

Q: Is there sort of a natural progression where you abide as awareness only?

S: There is no natural progression of awareness. Awareness is always here and now. But there can be a natural reduction in the influence that thoughts, feelings and sensations have on your experience.

When you've tried everything you can think of to take control of your life, and nothing has worked, you may sit down by yourself and look for the me that you assume you are. You'll look for the ego, the controlling entity you believed yourself to be, and you'll find nothing! There is no ego, no me, no controlling entity there. If you were a controlling entity, wouldn't you have taken control of your life years ago? There is no one there. Seeing this clearly, there is a sense of relief, peace, and ease that results.

At this point, it's still possible and not uncommon for doubts and contradictory thoughts to arise even after seeing this. But now you know there is no controlling entity there to control those thoughts; so doubts, fears, and contradictory thoughts float by like dead leaves in a fall breeze. You notice them, but you remain unconcerned and unaffected.

Q: I guess I am to notice more and more that there is awareness first before anything else?

S: Notice awareness right now. Are you aware? Awareness is always here and now, and you are awareness. That summarizes the entire teaching in one sentence! This understanding can be your daily experience.

34

The Recognition is Not Happening

Question: The recognition is not happening, so what can I do?

Stephen: Are you aware right now? There's nothing else to recognize.

Q: Jim is very real, this body is real, and the world is very separate to me.

S: Awareness is primary. Jim and the world are secondary. Do Jim and the world exist if you are not there to witness them? So, what is your essential nature: awareness, or Jim and his world?

Q: I don't see how I'm supposed to stop paying attention to thoughts and pay attention to this 'simplicity of being'.

S: Paying attention to thoughts is not a problem unless you believe in them. Nothing can trouble you but your own imagination. Is that true?

Q: I don't have any control or ability to stop paying attention to thought and to pay attention to the simplicity of my being.

S: Are you aware right now? What control or ability is required to know that you are aware right now?

Q: Trying is of the ego anyway so that can't be it.

S: Are you trying to be aware? Try *not* to be aware. Can you get away from awareness?

Q: No wonder no one gets this stuff, either grace does it or it doesn't.

S: There's nothing to get. Is grace required for you to be aware? This is just more conceptual nonsense.

Q: This awareness brings no knowledge, right? The thoughts of an awake person are no more valid or true that an unawake one? So any thoughts on cosmology are all just imagination? Like Yogananda's description of astral worlds and such?

S: What does awareness know? Thoughts, ideas, and beliefs are mind-stuff, and can be discussed and debated ad nauseum. Your existence as awareness cannot be debated. Awareness is always here and now. Your essential nature is awareness. There is only one thought that can be spoken which you cannot deny—that is 'I am'.

35

How Do You Get Beyond the Mind?

Question: In your correspondence entitled *Is There A Natural Progression?* You wrote the following: *'When you've tried everything you can think of to take control of your life, and nothing has worked, you may sit down by yourself and look for the me that you assume you are. You'll look for the ego, the controlling entity you believed yourself to be, and you'll find nothing!'*

I get somewhat frustrated when I read this kind of thing. How come when I look for the ego (separate self) I find one? It seems to be a gestalt of feeling, sensation, thought, memory, *and* awareness.

Stephen: Feelings, sensations, thoughts, and memories arise and fall. What must *always* be here to witness them: awareness, right? So, what is your *essential* nature: feelings, sensations, thoughts, and memories—or awareness? What is the ego or separate self that you find? Is it in control? Is it a problem? It's not in control, nor is it a problem, is it?

Q: I have also read that the answer is beyond the mind, but how do you get beyond the mind?

S: The mind is the thinking process. Can you get beyond the thinking process? What are you? The mind arises in you, right? Are you the thinking process, or are you aware of the thinking process? Make this practical right now. These words represent thoughts. Do you see them? Do you see your own thoughts arising in response to these words? Thoughts are arising in you now, right? Are you aware of the thoughts, the thinking process, which is the mind? Yes? You are beyond the mind now. You have always been beyond the mind!

Right now, experience yourself as awareness. Notice your surroundings; notice the chair you're sitting in; the sounds in the background; the temperature of the room; the thoughts that arise; the sensations in the body. You are pure awareness. Awareness is not a thought, feeling or sensation. Awareness cannot be grasped by the mind or body. The mind and body arise in awareness. The body and mind are always changing. Awareness is always here and now, unchanged, unaffected, and peaceful. Knowing yourself as awareness, *right now*, you know yourself as the peace that you were seeking by using your mind. There is no peace in the mind. There is no problem with awareness.

36

Give Yourself Two Weeks

Question: Part of the problem is that I have always considered awareness to be an attribute of mind. In non-duality circles, the definition of the mind seems to be only 'thought'. Yes, feelings, thoughts and memories are included in the awareness. But awareness seems to come and go, too, as the mind gets lost in a train of thought.

Stephen: Is there ever a time when you can say, 'Awareness is gone now?' Even when your focus is on the train of thought, is awareness gone? It is not possible for awareness to come and go. Try to make awareness go away. You are awareness. What comes and goes is the thought 'I am aware now'. The thought 'I am aware now' is not awareness.

Q: The ego seems to have minimal control. I can try to do things, and sometimes it seems to work, sometimes it doesn't. Even when it doesn't, though, and I'm not in control, that seems to be a problem, because then I feel I have to try harder.

S: You did not control your birth. You will not control your death. And you are not in control of anything in between. Enlightenment is seeing that there is no separate, controlling entity there in you, no ego—no one who can be enlightened, and realizing that what you are in essence is awareness. By the way, *you* are not trying harder; trying harder is happening.

Q: Even when I can see that the thinking is included in the awareness, and that what I am is awareness, the awareness I am still seems to have problems. For instance, I have been working very hard lately, which makes me tired and anxious. Tiredness and anxiety therefore exist within awareness. The awareness *is* tiredness and anxiety.

S: Tiredness and anxiety are states of mind. The mind is the thinking process. Awareness is neither tired nor rested, neither anxious nor at ease. Awareness just is. When the thought 'I am tired and anxious' does not arise, is there any such thing as tiredness or anxiety?

Q: What is odd about this kind of dialogue is that my questions seem to be defensive and argumentative, but I have no problem at all with what you're saying. I'm just trying to experience it, rather than just intellectually agree with it.

S: Give yourself two weeks to get to the bottom of this and make the intellectual understanding become your experience. Find out for yourself, in your own direct experience, what is your essential nature—not conceptually, but experientially. Are you the ego? Are you in control of your life and experience? Are you the controller? Or are you pure awareness?

The idea of being a separate, controlling entity (ego) is the root of all suffering. Get to the bottom of it. Are you in control? Yes or no? Not maybe or sometimes a little bit—*Yes or no?* Are you aware? Yes or no? Again, not maybe or sometimes a little bit—*Yes or no?*

Q: I assume you went through the same thing yourself, and wish you could somehow relay to me how you got from identifying with the separate self to seeing that you are not separate.

S: Do you see that there is no such thing as oneness? Seeing there is no such thing as oneness, you see there is no such thing as separation. Separation and oneness are both concepts. Awareness is not a concept. You are awareness.

Q: There are moments when I feel I am directly experiencing reality, when there is a kind of stillness and what is seems to take on an extra dimension. But even then it is the separate self that is having an experience. I have only rarely glimpsed the feeling of no self. Oddly enough, it sometimes happens when I look in the mirror and see the reflection as 'not me'.

S: You cannot experience reality; there are no extra dimensions; there is no separate self who has an experience of stillness; there is no feeling of no self—there is no such thing as reality. The anecdotes you've cited sound good, but upon investigation they're recognized as conceptual nonsense.

37

Keep Asking Questions Until They're Burned Away

Question: Every time I notice, I see I am aware. But the body, mind, and all that goes with it, are also very real.

Stephen: Your body exists as a flowing series of sensations: some painful, some pleasurable. Your mind exists as a flowing series of thoughts: some happy, some sad. To say that you are not the body and mind, or they are not real is not quite true. However, your body and mind are not your essential nature, and they are not problematic. You are not in control of your body and mind. Your body and mind are functioning on their own. The body and mind become problematic only when there is a belief that you are in control of them. You are not in control of anything at all. In fact, there is no separate, controlling entity there in your body or mind. Whatever sensations or thoughts that arise in your body and mind have arisen on their own. The Source of all of existence including your body, mind, thoughts and sensations is a mystery. Some call it God, Intelligence, Universal Life, the Buddha Mind. Whichever word we use, the Source is an absolute mystery.

Q: I'm trying to focus more and more on awareness. Should there be a feeling of peace? There is no knowing of freedom. It seems there is still limitation.

S: Where you find peace there is the potential for war. Where you find freedom, there is the potential for bondage. You are not in control of the peace or the war. You are not in control of the freedom or the bondage. You are not in control of anything at all. *You do not exist as a separate, controlling entity!* When the sense of personal doer-ship is seen as false, you know yourself as awareness only. This awareness is the peace that is at peace with war. This awareness is the freedom that is free even when bound.

Q: I've read of the following: this awareness is ever fresh, ever new (not known here), boundless peace (not recognized here), an awareness that sparkles (not recognized here). I know that those who know are a 100% convinced, and I can sense the truth of what they say; yet here there is only plain, ordinary awareness!

S: There are many terms that are used to describe awareness. You've probably heard the terms emptiness and fullness. Both are correct. How can that be? Awareness is neither empty nor full. Awareness can be referred to as sparkling and light, or deep and dark. Again, both are correct, but awareness is neither light nor dark.

If you've found a description of awareness that appeals to you such as ever fresh and new, sparkling or peaceful, and you look for that description, you'll be frustrated! Awareness is, period. It is neither ordinary nor extraordinary. It just is. Anything that can be described is not awareness.

Q: I don't know what else to say (sounds like a lot of complaints by the ego and I know that is what it is)!

S: Complaints, doubts, and concerns are arising in the form of thoughts. Thoughts are dead. They are irrelevant. I don't believe any of your thoughts, do you? By the way, there is no such thing as an ego. It's just another thought.

Q: Yet, there is no conviction here that I Am That!

S: You are aware. Is any conviction needed? Keep asking whatever questions you have. You may be very close to having all your questions burned away. You won't believe it when you see how simple this really is. You'll look back and ask yourself how you could have missed something that's been apparent all of your life, and is so simple and obvious. You may laugh so hard that your stomach will hurt. That's what happened to me. Don't give up—you're at the door.

38

What's Holding You Back From Seeing This?

Question: The frustration level here has dimmed considerably. There is only a feeling of resignation I just shrug my shoulders and say 'this is how it is now'. Alas, there is still so much identification with thought. Anyway, if you can offer your assessment of my current situation based on our correspondence, please feel free to do so.

Stephen: Here's my sense of what your experience has been: based on your questions thus far, it seems that your focus has been on your expectations of what the understanding may bring to your experience. Understandably, it seems you are looking for an experience of peace and freedom. You want to be free of your identification with thought, and see the body and mind as unreal or as 'not me'. And you want the peaceful, easy experience of knowing yourself as awareness and not a separate ego.

These expectations are perfectly reasonable based on what you've read and heard during your spiritual search. After all, that's the description of the enlightened state that has been written and talked about for thousands of years. I, too, use terms like these in my writings. At some point in time, maybe right now, you'll see that all of the words, all of the talk, all of the descriptions that create expectations of peace, joy, and freedom are just words, concepts, ideas, and beliefs.

You'll realize that your search for the enlightened state was an absolute joke. You'll see that the only truth you know for certain is that you exist, you are aware—you are awareness itself. You'll see that your expectations that were fostered by the writings and talks about the enlightened state were off the mark. Awareness is so simple and fundamental that any attempt to describe it creates false expectations that lead to frustration and disappointment.

Awareness is—period. Your existence as awareness is what's being pointed out. Awareness always is. The content of awareness is not important. The content of awareness may be peaceful or disturbing; it may be light and easy, or heavy and dark; it may be pleasurable or painful. But awareness always is. The content of awareness is always changing. Any attempt to grasp onto or avoid the content of awareness is fruitless and frustrating.

You are awareness. Knowing yourself as awareness, not its content, you are at peace with whatever arises. Know yourself as awareness, and your search is over. Are you awareness, or are you its content?

Continue asking questions until they're burned away. What's left when the questions are gone is what you've been searching for, what's always been here. Not because your questions were answered, but because you've seen them to be irrelevant and off the mark. You've seen that you are pure awareness, and nothing else really matters. Let's get to the bottom of it, and you'll be through with your search for good. You may even find yourself sharing the freedom you've discovered with others! So, is anything else holding you back from seeing this?

39

Death and Reincarnation

Question: When I asked you about reincarnation you said, 'What reincarnates?' I take it to be your view that there's nothing to reincarnate; hence, it doesn't happen.

Stephen: Having an opinion about reincarnation is not necessary to live in peace.

Q: If you just tell me I'm awareness and I don't see it, then there's no reason to communicate further, and I'm just as lost as before. Of course all this mind-stuff is pointless to you, but don't you have to reach me where I am?

S: That's exactly where I'm trying to reach you, at 'I am' period. I'm pointing to where you are, here and now. Your questions show your interest is in anything but here and now. When you are more interested in yourself as 'I am', here and now; and less interested in 'I was' or 'I will be', our communications may help you realize you are not lost, you've always been home.

Q: Did you read the article on reincarnation I sent to you? If you and the author of the article are both awareness itself, then why aren't you agreeing about reincarnation?

S: Agreeing or disagreeing about reincarnation can be entertaining as an intellectual debate. But, again, your focus on reincarnation shows an interest in 'I was' and 'I will be'. My interest is in pointing you to yourself as 'I am'. There is no peace in 'I was' or 'I will be'. There is no problem in 'I am'.

Q: So death brings instant enlightenment? With the death of the body and mind it's bingo, game over?

S: Who becomes enlightened? Who dies? Do you die every night when you go to sleep? Do you reincarnate every morning when you wake up?

Q: One of my favorite teachers says the only reason to talk about this is that we all do not go to the same place at death. That makes sense to me.

S: What do *you* say about death, reincarnation, and enlightenment? What do *you* want to get out of talking about all of this? If you're interested in living in peace in this lifetime, then questions about death, reincarnation, and enlightenment are irrelevant. Knowing yourself as 'I am' is all that's necessary.

Awareness Is the I AM THAT I AM

Question: You have hit the conceptual nail on its head! The moment I read your email there was a strong knowing that this was exactly what's been happening here. [See correspondence entitled *What's Holding You Back From Seeing This*] There have been times when there's a knowing that this is awareness, and the only thing that can be said is that awareness is, period. That's not to say that other times it has not been there, it's just that there's been so much identification with mind and thought that it's been overlooked. Yet, there is still a doubt that maybe this is not it?

Stephen: You said, 'There have been times when there's a knowing that this is awareness, and the only thing that can be said is that awareness is, period'. Yes, That *is* it! Awareness is, period. And you are awareness! You can spend another ten, twenty, or thirty years reading, searching, struggling and seeking enlightenment, and this is what you'll find: awareness is!

Awareness is what's being pointed out here. The content of awareness is *not* important. You may have heard of the neti-neti approach to which Nisargadatta and others refer. Neti-neti means 'not this, not this'. Anything that arises in awareness is not awareness. A doubt arises in the form of the thought 'maybe this is not it'. This thought is just content of awareness and is unimportant—neti-neti! Even the thought 'this *is* it' is just content and is unimportant—neti-neti! *All* thoughts are neti-neti. Awareness always is!

Awareness is so fundamental and simple that this recognition can be overlooked and rejected as too simple. Do not reject this now! It is this simple. You are home! *Your* awareness is what all the ancient traditions are pointing to. Awareness is the I AM THAT I AM. You are That. You've always been and always will be That. Awareness cannot be attained. Awareness cannot be lost. You are awareness. If any doubts arise, let's clear them out. You can be finished with your search right now. There is no need to struggle with this anymore.

41

Sidetracked By the Inessentials

Question: Well, I'm just not seeing it, and I don't know what other questions to ask about waking up. I can't make it happen. There's no one here to do it or not, right? Since a great curiosity exists, I ask other questions. At least maybe I can know a little about it. I want to wake up, but don't see how. So, what now? I'm sure the guys sitting with Ramana for thirty years talked about everything. You make it sound like I have a choice to wake up or not. I don't see it.

Stephen: I just now re-read all of our email communications thus far, and I'm going to make a suggestion to you based on that. Stick with the basics. The fundamental truth expressed in the non-dual traditions is 'Consciousness is all there is, and I Am That'.

The critical question you need to answer in your own direct experience is 'Who or what am I?' Ponder over these questions related to finding out who or what you are. What is awareness? Who am I? What is my essential nature? Can thoughts, feelings, and sensations exist without awareness being here to witness them? What is this sense of being-ness that I feel right now? Am I aware?

For now, drop all other questions about death, reincarnation, free will, destiny, grace, enlightenment, waking up, astral worlds, and quotes from 'enlightened' teachers. Answer the question, 'Who am I?' not conceptually, but in your own direct experience. No one can do this for you. You must see it for yourself. Answering the question, 'Who am I?' will put all other questions into proper perspective.

If you're serious about this, then give yourself two weeks to get to the bottom of it. Stick with the basics, and you'll see this in no time. If you get sidetracked by the inessentials, you can spend the rest of your life in the mind.

42

Is There Free Will or Does Destiny Rule?

Question: I like your statements to the effect that all I know for certain is that I am, and everything else is a complete mystery. This resonates with the way I see things, and resolves a lot of my confusion generated by Advaita teachings.

Stephen: Yes, right now you know you exist, I am. This 'I am' we can call consciousness. So, we can say, 'consciousness is'. The fact that 'consciousness is' cannot be denied—everything else is debatable.

Q: There seem to be a lot of Advaita teachings that I do not understand, but that are crucial to the end of suffering. But these teachings seem like so much baggage to me.

S: The fundamental teaching of Advaita can be summed up by saying, 'All there is, is consciousness, and I am That'. Knowing yourself as consciousness, and not a separate, controlling entity, suffering comes to an end along with the sufferer.

Eating from the tree of the knowledge of good and evil (identifying with, believing in, and exercising the discriminating mind), we suffer. Having only the knowledge of our own existence as I am, consciousness, there is no suffering, no sufferer, and no baggage.

Q: The saying, 'there is doing but no doer', what the heck does that mean? I could take it to mean I am not a noun, but a verb. Not a thing but a process. And then that process is seen to be interconnected with the total process of the universe.

S: Well put!

Q: The process of a flame is interconnected with its environment. Material elements enter the process, get transformed, and by-products leave the process—all continuous with the totality of the environment. But the flame is still a flame. By analogy, a person is a process, not separate from its environment. But it is still a person. It is alive, while its environment is not alive.

S: We can say that the flame and the person exist as concepts, but they have no independent existence. There is no entity that is separate from the universal process. The universe is one. You and the flame are the universe.

Is the universe actually divided by thought? Labeling the burning process 'flame' does not separate the flame from the universal process. Labeling the human process a 'person' does not separate the person from the universal process. There is one process, one universe, one consciousness, and you are that.

Q: These seem to be two equally valid ways of looking at it: the whole and the parts, the One and the many. It's an absolute mystery. Why should one view be more important than the other? And yet, according to Advaita, the view from the One is the absolute view, and is how suffering gets removed.

S: Psychological suffering gets removed by seeing and knowing that you are not a separate, controlling person who must struggle and fight to be at peace in the world; and seeing and knowing that what you are in essence is the awareness that is always here and now, always at peace with whatever arises. Knowing yourself as consciousness, I am, you are the peace that is at peace with war.

Q: Another dualism is free will versus determinism (the absence of free will). Philosophers seem to accept both views as equally valid even though they are contradictory. In other words, it's a complete mystery. Yet Advaita says there is no free will. No free will also contradicts another Advaita teaching, that what we are is absolute freedom. If we *are* absolute freedom, how can we have no free will?

S: The absolute freedom that we are, I am, has nothing to do with the concepts of free will or determinism. Free will and determinism are interesting concepts that are entertaining to discuss and debate, but it's not necessary to have an opinion about them to live in peace.

Just for the entertainment value, consider these questions: if we have free will, can we choose determinism instead? Is there a person who is separate from the universal process who can exercise free will? If there's still a clinging to the concept of free will, then go ahead and exercise your free will—choose only happy thoughts and feelings for the next two weeks. Of what value is free will if it cannot be exercised?

In this I AM THAT I AM, there is neither free will nor destiny; and there is both free will and destiny. Is there free will or does destiny rule? All I know for certain is that I am. This I am is the peace that's being sought by exercising the intellect with questions about free will and destiny. Know yourself as I am right now and your search is over.

43

Why the Doubts?

Question: There is still this doubt: am I recognizing what is being pointed to clearly, and if so, then why the doubts? I know that every doubt is a thought arising in awareness, but I'm questioning if I know myself as awareness clearly?

Stephen: It's quite common to have doubts arise. They don't mean anything, and they will subside. You know you exist as awareness otherwise you could not witness the arising of doubts or anything else.

Sitting at your desk reading these words right now there is a seeing that's happening through your eyes. Slow down right now and be aware of the seeing. Hearing is happening through your ears, are you aware of the hearing? Do you feel your body sitting there in the chair? Are you aware of the seeing, the hearing, and the senses of your body sitting there now? You are the awareness of the seeing, hearing, and sensing.

Different objects appear in your seeing, hearing, and sensing. But you are always the awareness. Without you, nothing can be seen, heard, or sensed. Doubts arise in the form of thoughts. Are you aware of the thoughts? You are the awareness of the doubts that arise in the form of thoughts. Different thoughts arise in awareness. But you are always awareness. Without you, no thoughts can arise.

This teaching points to your essential nature as awareness. You are awareness. Without you nothing exists. You are always awareness. You are always here and now. It's not possible for you to be anything other than awareness, or any place or time other than here and now. You are not affected by doubts.

Your experience is quite common. I'm happy to correspond with you until you laugh at all your doubts

This Koan Called Advaita

Question: I've been reading and thinking a lot about this Advaita, non-duality stuff. Sometimes I feel that I get it, and other times I'm frustrated. I think I have some blocks to understanding it, and I'm wondering whether non-duality or oneness is true?

Stephen: The concepts of Advaita may be the ultimate Zen koan. Trying to understand the concepts to determine if the premise of non-duality is true is bound to leave you frustrated. The more you study Advaita, the more contradictory concepts you'll find.

Struggling to understand this koan called Advaita may expose the limits of the intellect. The realization may come that all concepts can be refuted, and that there's no way to know anything for certain. This recognition may lead to what J. Krishnamurti refers to as the 'Freedom from the Known'. The 'known' refers to concepts, knowledge, the thinking process—all of which is the mind. Being free of the known does not mean that the thinking process (the mind) is no longer active, but it's seen that all concepts can be refuted or denied. Clearly seeing this leaves one in a 'Cloud of Unknowing' as the 14th century, anonymous, Christian mystic put it. And my favorite, Nisargadatta Maharaj, when discussing his realization in the book *I AM THAT*, said this about understanding and knowledge:

'I found myself desiring and knowing less and less, until I could say in utter astonishment: 'I know nothing, I want nothing.' Earlier I was sure of so many things, now I am sure of nothing. But I feel I have lost nothing by not knowing, because all my knowledge was false. My not knowing was in itself knowledge of the fact that all knowledge is ignorance, that 'I do not know' is the only true statement the mind can make'.

The ultimate understanding of Advaita is non-conceptual. The ultimate understanding is 'Consciousness is all there is, and I am that'.

Q: From your essay entitled *Bottom Line: How Does This Work?* You said, 'If you are not conscious can anything else exist?' Doesn't stuff happen regardless of whether someone perceives it? For example, the refrigerator still exists even when I leave the kitchen. Am I misunderstanding what you're saying? Things do exist independently of someone perceiving or experiencing them, right?

S: Answer this question right now in your own direct experience, not from a theoretical perspective: if you are not conscious right now, can anything else exist for you? Philosophers and physicists have the pleasure (and the frustration) of attempting to describe consciousness with concepts. Some say the perceiver, the perceiving, and the perceived are one. This 'one' is consciousness. Therefore, consciousness is all there is.

My interest in this is practical, not philosophical. Seeing that nothing can trouble you but your own imagination leaves you free of psychological suffering.

Q: My next question is related to the previous one. I think I've had the experience of being simply aware, and I think I understand what you're referring to when you say, 'Notice the awareness of the seeing. This awareness is what you are'. But there is confusion when you say 'without this awareness nothing else exists'. Can you explain what you mean by this?

S: Awareness is always here and now. The objects of awareness are always changing. Awareness is primary. The objects of awareness are secondary. Without awareness, can any object be witnessed?

Again, my interest in this is practical not theoretical or philosophical. Most of my adult life, I experienced psychological suffering. I was completely identified with my thoughts, my story, my life, my drama, my suffering. At the root of my suffering was the belief that I was the mind, the thinking process, the ego, the controller or guide of Stephen's life. After years and years of struggling, suffering, and seeking, these simple pointers struck home: I am not a separate controlling entity, I am awareness, period. Consciousness is all there is, and I am That.

The recognition that my essential nature is pure awareness, and not a separate, controlling entity snapped my identification with the mind, its stories and dramas, and its incessant, yet failed attempts at controlling my life. When the identification with the mind snapped, so did the attempt to control my life experience. So now life goes on as it always has. Everything is as it is—the good, the bad, and the ugly. But with the realization that struggling with what is, is futile, even struggling with the struggling!

As Paul put it in the New Testament, 'I live, yet not I, but Christ lives in me'. Paul's words apply to all of us, whether it's realized or not.

Q: From your correspondence entitled *Make This Observation* you say the following:

'It's easy to see and feel that your heart is beating, but you are not beating your heart. It's easy to realize that your eyes are seeing, your ears are hearing, your lungs are breathing, and you are not doing any of it. But for some reason, for those of us who have suffered, there is the sense that we are in control of our thoughts, feelings, and actions'.

You mention that we don't control the seeing, hearing, heart beating or thinking, but isn't it true that we do have some control? We can control when we see (we can close our eyes), what we see (by looking here or there). This also applies to the other senses and physical functions. I appreciate the fact that there are limits to how much we can alter our physical functions, but don't we have some control? And doesn't this imply that there is a 'someone' who is doing the choosing and controlling, albeit limited?

S: Are you in control of anything at all? The thought arises to close your eyes, so you close your eyes. Did you create the thought that says close your eyes? The thought 'look over there' arises, so you look over there. Choices are made and thoughts arise. Is there a separate, controlling entity there in you who makes choices and thinks thoughts?

If you believe there's an entity there who is in control of your thoughts, then go ahead and exercise that control. Why would you ever choose an unhappy thought if you were in control? Believing that you are a separate, controlling entity is at the root of psychological suffering. Knowing yourself as awareness, here and now, you are free of psychological suffering.

45

Is Psychological Suffering Just a Bad Idea?

Question: I read one of your writings in which you say that suffering is 'just a bad idea!' Could you please convince me of this?

Stephen: Look into these questions about suffering from your own personal experience. Write your answers in your own words, from your own perspective, describe your own suffering. Clearly seeing the process of your own personal suffering will help shed some light on this subject.

What's happening when you're experiencing suffering?
Who or what is at the root of your psychological suffering?
What is awareness?
What is your essential nature?

Q: You will say that I am consciousness and not a person. I understand this with the mind but to live this, as the truth, is quite another matter. Could you please help me with this problem which is of course still of the ego? Maybe there should be more awareness?

S: Awareness is always here and now. Awareness does not increase or decrease. Thoughts, feelings, sensations, stories, and people all come and go. Does awareness ever come and go? Is your essential nature a thought, a feeling, a sensation, a story, or a person—or is your essential nature consciousness? Look into these questions deeply from your own personal experience, and you may find a sense of relief from psychological suffering. It worked for me.

Agnosticism: The One True Faith?

Question: I kind of get it. Being fully present, that's all there is.

Stephen: It's not that you need to be fully present, it's that you *are* presence-awareness. Notice your presence as awareness right now.

Q: When I think of non-dual concepts like 'time is mind and mind is time', I get lost.

S: Notice this now: You are here and now, existing as awareness, and the thought arises, 'time is mind and mind is time. I'm lost'. You, awareness, are here before, during, and after that thought arose. You, awareness, are always here and now. No thoughts can arise, nothing can exist unless you, awareness, are here to witness it. Do you see this?
   Awareness is not a thought; it's not a concept. Awareness need not be understood like a concept, but simply noticed. Notice it now. You cannot get lost. Conflicting thoughts may arise. The thought, 'I am lost' may arise. But awareness, you, is always here witnessing the thought, 'I am lost'. Is awareness ever lost?

Q: I can appreciate that there is no problem unless I think about it, but it's difficult not to think about it! A lot of mind-stuff seems really enjoyable too! Like anticipating a holiday, catching up with friends, enjoying a good film.

S: Your world and experiences are thought-based. And the central thought around which all your experiences revolve is the thought 'I'. When the thought 'I' arises the world arises. You may notice this when you wake up in the morning. The first thought upon awakening starts with 'I', and then you and your stories arise. There's no problem with it, unless you believe it's true. Clearly seeing this, you're more likely to enjoy your holidays, friends, and watching a good film.
   Also, whether you're thinking about problems or not is not the issue, but seeing that problems are nothing more than thoughts is the key. Seeing that problems are just thoughts, suffering over them ceases.

Q: Damn! If this non-duality stuff is the real deal, why do so few people get it? There are some scathing critiques of it, too. I don't really feel knowledgeable enough to judge the critique or the object of the criticism. It just makes me believe more firmly in the one true faith: agnosticism!

S: The essential pointer of non-duality is this: 'Consciousness is, and you are that'. Can you deny your own existence? Can consciousness be critiqued? Do you need to be knowledgeable to realize that you exist, you are aware? All the other concepts of non-duality are just pointers to that one fact.

An agnostic realizes he doesn't know if God exists. But you know *you* exist, right? You don't need to believe that you exist, you know you exist. You can express the fact of your own existence by saying, 'I am'. Many religious scriptures refer to God as I AM, or I AM THAT I AM. No belief is required. Why don't more people get this? It's because they're using their intellect to try to get it. If there's anything to get, it's the fact that there's nothing to get. Your own existence, your own being, awareness, consciousness is not something you can get. You are it.

Q: The growing popularity of Advaita seems to be helping people, but I wonder if it's objectively true? I reckon it would be difficult to accept that 'time is a meaningless concept' or 'nothing exists outside of your being aware of it'.

S: You need not accept those concepts. Just recognize your own existence as awareness. Are you, awareness, either true or false? Concepts can be true or false, but you are not a concept.

Q: Interesting that Sri Nisargadatta recommends meditation when so many non-dual teachers think it's a hindrance?

S: In the book, *I AM THAT*, Nisargadatta offers pointers to the fact of our own being. To some he may suggest meditation or inquiry, and to others he may say meditation and inquiry are unnecessary. In my opinion, his goal is to point seekers to their own essence as awareness, not to be consistent with any method or concepts of non-duality.

Panic Attacks

Question: I resonate with what you say about the natural state. At first I was excited about this discovery that there is *no one here*, and I experienced real peace, joy and happiness. But now there's this sense of inner panic—not all the time, but a lot of the time. Is that my ego rebelling? Have others experienced this state of panic? I would really appreciate your view on this 'panic' state.

Stephen: Panic and panic attacks are not uncommon. I can speak about this from my own personal experience. Others have shared their experiences with this, too. [See correspondence entitled *What Can I Expect to Get Out of This*] I suffered for several years from panic attacks that caused psychological and physical suffering. By observing the process of fear and panic in my own experience, and seeing that nothing can trouble me but my own imagination, I no longer experience them.

Let's take a look at the process of fear and panic. Fear arises in response to a sense of danger or threat. On a biological level, fear is a natural survival mechanism. When a poisonous snake or a rabid dog crosses your path, a sense of danger and fear arise, and you take the appropriate action to avoid being harmed. When the threat has been averted, the sense of danger and fear pass and you go about your business.

Panic is an intense, exaggerated sense of fear that is more psychological than biological in essence. Fear turns to panic when the imagination conjures up horrible images and stories about how terrible things will happen to me if I can't deal with a perceived threat. When fear and panic become more frequent and intense, physical symptoms such as headache, heart palpitations, and fainting may occur. It can become so problematic that you panic about the *possibility* of having a panic attack in the *future*. So it's a vicious cycle of fear, imagination and panic.

When you're experiencing a psychological panic attack, there are two underlying assumptions. The first one is that there's a me, an ego, an independent, separate person who can be harmed, and who must take action to avoid being harmed. And second, there's a belief that the imaginary threat is real. So have a look and see if you can find an independent, separate, controlling entity there in you. Find out for yourself if there is a 'psychological you' who can be harmed. Find out what you are in essence. The physical body can be harmed, but can you be harmed? Nothing can trouble you but your own imagination. Is that true?

Fear arises as a natural response to a threat to your body, the biological organism, and there's no problem with that. The body will take care of itself. But if you're experiencing psychological suffering and panic attacks, it's possible to be free of them by observing the process and discovering that there is no independent, separate entity, no ego, no me who can be harmed.

So the next time a panic attack arises, ask yourself if you're really at risk of being harmed, and is anything real troubling you or is it just imagination? It's possible to be free of all sorts of psychological suffering, including panic attacks.

48

Attention vs. Awareness

Question: What's the difference between attention and awareness? I've heard some say that attention is a tool of the mind, and others say that attention is an aspect of awareness. Please clarify.

Stephen: We could say that awareness, which is the absolute, has the capacity to create and be conscious of the relative through the function of the mind, which is the thinking process. Attention is awareness functioning as the mind. Ultimately there is no real difference. Awareness is all there is, and you are that!

We could use this analogy: when sunlight passes through a prism, the individual colors can be seen. The sunlight is awareness, the prism is the mind or attention, and the colors are the relative appearance. Ultimately, all are awareness.

49

Fed-Up With Seeking!

Question: I just must stop, ugh, seeking, ugh! I find it difficult to articulate my queries. I am wary of falling into mental concepts since even the very idea that I've understood something seems to be faulty. I keep thinking I know what Nisargadatta is talking about, but upon reviewing what I think I've understood, I find that I've completely driven this so-called understanding toward a mental interpretation that's convenient for whatever state of mind I'm in.

Stephen: The final understanding is non-conceptual. Awareness is not a concept. Are you aware right now? This awareness is what you are. Any mental interpretation takes place in the your awareness, here and now. Even the frustration of 'trying to get it' takes place in your awareness, here and now. The excitement of feeling 'I get it' takes place in your awareness, here and now. Awareness is always here and now, unaffected by any thoughts or feelings of getting it or losing it.

Q: A history of thirty years of thinking I've understood (sometimes using intense seeking techniques) and knowing that I've not understood anything gives me no self-confidence at all that this time around I'll 'get it'.

S: If there's anything to get, it's the fact that there's nothing to get. Using intense seeking techniques implies there's something you're missing, and applying the intense seeking technique will give you something you don't already have. Awareness is what you are. While all of the seeking and searching is happening, awareness is here witnessing the whole event.

Q: For example, the statement 'you are already it' is an obvious confirmation of what must be true: what else could I be? But it's not my living reality. I don't get it!

S: The 'it' in the statement, 'you are already it', is awareness, and you say it's not your living reality. I'm suggesting you take another look. It is indeed your living reality. You are awareness.

Q: I'll consider my questions more carefully and see if I can hone them down.

S: What is my essential nature? What is awareness? Am I in control of thoughts, feelings and sensations? Am I a separate, controlling entity? These questions point directly to what you are, and help you clearly see what you are not. Your seeking will come to an end when you see there's nothing you can attain, nothing you need to understand, and nothing anyone can give you. Your seeking will come to an end when you see that your essential nature, awareness, is the peace that you're seeking, and it's already here. See it now!

50

Any Additional Pointers?

Question: It's been a while since I last contacted you. Things seem to be letting up here. There seems to be a sort of ease in living, but is that the mind again? When disturbing thoughts arise, there seems to be a knowing that this is only a thought, and there is recognition of that, too, as a thought (if that makes sense). Anyway, I'd like to hear from you if you have any additional pointers.

Stephen: You have a solid understanding of all that needs to be seen. You know your essential nature is consciousness. You know that you are not a separate, controlling entity. You know that nothing can trouble you but your own imagination.

You've seen clearly that thoughts, feelings, and sensations all come and go in you. You've seen and understood all that you are not: body, senses and mind. Now just be aware of awareness. You are awareness. Awareness is freedom itself. You are freedom itself. Thoughts, feelings, and sensations all come and go. Pay no attention to them—there is no peace in them. Notice your own awareness. Notice your essence as awareness. Notice that you, awareness, are always here and now. There is no problem with awareness; there is no freedom in the body and mind. You are not the body and mind. You are free of the body and mind.

When disturbing, thoughts, feelings or sensations arise, notice that they pass, and you, awareness, always remain. Now that you have this understanding, just be aware of awareness. Notice the sense of beingness. Notice that your eyes are seeing, your ears are hearing, all of your senses are active, and you are aware! You are free. You are freedom itself.

51

From Concepts to Living Experience

Question: I'm fifty-five years old, and over the years I've lived in monasteries, ashrams, and communes. I've spent time with the Krishna's and the Sikhs; been to India three times, and studied the teachings of Advaita. These past six months I've been reading, watching, and listening to various non-duality teachers' books, DVDs and CDs.

On your website you wrote the following: *'When it is realized that we are not the limited person we had taken ourselves to be, and that we are the awareness of all that is, then the ultimate understanding becomes our living experience'.* I'd like this to be my living experience. Can you help me?

Stephen: It's possible for the intellectual understanding to become your living experience. After reading hundreds of books on spirituality and religious philosophy, talking with and listening to dozens of teachers over the years, listening to CDs and DVDs it all comes down to this: all we know for certain is that consciousness is, I am.

If you're interested in happiness without sadness, pleasure without pain, you're guaranteed to suffer. Consciousness is. You are. I am. Happiness and sadness, pleasure and pain all come and go as experiences in awareness. Even the 'I am' comes and goes in awareness.

Are you in control of your experiences of happiness and sadness, pleasure and pain? There is no separate, controlling entity there in you or me who can control our experiences. If you believe there is, then go ahead and exercise your control, and choose only happiness from now on. There is no separate ego who can control anything at all. All there is, is consciousness, awareness, and this is what you are. Find out for your self if this is true.

Happiness and sadness are not problematic unless there's an unexamined belief that you, the ego, the controller of your life, can take action to avoid sadness and hold onto happiness—this is suffering, the resistance to what is. When you see that you don't exist as a separate, controlling entity there is a sense of relief, a surrendering that happens. You can't surrender because you don't exist as a separate controller. Have you ever *tried* to surrender? It doesn't work. But seeing that there's no way you can do it, seeing there is no 'you' who can do it, it's possible for it to happen.

If you are not a separate controlling entity an ego, then what are you? What do you know about yourself that cannot be denied? Certainly you know that you exist, I am. What is this sense of being that you are? When are you? Where are you? What are you? You exist. Consciousness is. I am—period! You are awareness itself. You are nothing but pure awareness. Stop right now and be aware of awareness. Everything else is imagination, and nothing can trouble you but your own imagination. This is what the teachers and ancient traditions are pointing out. Look for yourself and find out if it's true for you, too.

52

Witness the Dissolution of the 'I'

Question: If I am awareness only, then doesn't that mean that everything is simply a movie in front of that.

Stephen: Yes, your essential nature is awareness. It can be an effective pointer to say that everything else is simply a movie happening upon you, awareness. You are not a separate person, ego, or controlling entity. There is no ego there in you controlling the movie that's playing out as your life experience. There is happiness and sadness, pleasure and pain, and all sorts of experiences happening. You are not the writer or director of the movie. We could say that you, as a person, are an actor who is playing his part in the universal movie. Your essential nature is awareness; you are not a separate, controlling entity. You are not the writer or director of your life story.

Q: That would mean there is nothing that can be done about it, and life will go on as before. Any action or thought that happens is just spontaneously happening.

S: Everything is happening spontaneously. I'm writing these words spontaneously, and you are reading them spontaneously. Doing happens spontaneously, but there's no separate doer. If there's a belief that you are a separate person, a separate doer, you may experience psychological suffering. And the desire to be free of psychological suffering will arise spontaneously. Then you hear the teaching of non-duality that says your essential nature is awareness, peaceful and free, so you spontaneously try to make this your living experience. You follow the suggestion to find out who or what you are in essence. And you recognize for yourself that your essential nature is pure awareness, and that you are not a separate person. Knowing your self as pure awareness, a sense of peace and freedom arises spontaneously.

Q: Is the only difference that there would be no belief in a person? It strikes me that it must be something more, to explain the joy and deep peace that is said to be felt.

S: Awareness, the inherent peace that you are, is causeless. It just is. Psychological suffering has a cause, and it can be eliminated. What's left? Awareness: causeless, beginning-less, endless, peaceful and free!

Q: Also, I still wouldn't be seeing things as all one; separation would still exist.

S: Separation is a function of the mind, which is the thinking process. It's the nature of thought to divide, label, categorize, and judge. You are awareness. The thinking process, which is the process of separation, cannot happen unless you, awareness, are here to witness it.

Notice that you, awareness, exist before, during, and after the thinking process. Notice your experience when you wake up tomorrow morning. The first thought you have will be 'I', and then your personal story will follow. What was there before the thought 'I' arose? Pure Awareness! Awareness is there and witnesses the first thought, the 'I' thought.

You can also witness the dissolution of the 'I' as you fall off to sleep at night. The world dissolves as the thinking process slows down, and your personal story narrows to just the sense of being, I am. And then even the 'I am' fades as consciousness goes to sleep. What's left? Pure awareness—life itself. This awareness is what you are in essence. You are life itself. You are the One! You cannot see things as one; *you are the One!* There is no separation.

Q: I'm also puzzled as to why the pointers talk of experiencing ourselves as awareness, noticing the sense of awareness, or abiding as that awareness. How is that possible, since awareness cannot see itself without making itself an object? Surely any experience of awareness is not it since awareness can't be experienced. You say 'pay attention to the awareness that you are'. If I could pay attention to it, wouldn't that make it an appearance?

S: Yes, indeed. That's why they're referred to as pointers only. Once it's realized that awareness is, period, all the pointers are discarded. Once you know yourself as awareness, any pointer that implies a separation between you and awareness is off the mark. When you know yourself as awareness, here and now, how can you, awareness, pay attention to, notice, abide as, or experience awareness? You are awareness. There is no separation.

The most direct pointers are simple: 'Consciousness Is' or 'I Am'. For some, that's all they need to recognize this. For others, additional pointers are needed. Most non-dual teachings are prefaced with a note about the pointers.

I used this one on my website on the Philosophy page: *'There are many words that can be used to describe non-duality, but the words are not the thing itself. All words are dual by nature; therefore, words can be used as pointers only'.*

Lao Tzu said 'the Tao that can be named is not the Eternal Tao'. He then proceeded to write the Tao Te Ching, attempting to describe or 'name' it. Such is the nature of language. So, Consciousness is!! Bye, bye!

How Will I Know the Understanding is Complete?

Question: I'm writing to give you an update, and follow up with a question or two. I've had two experiences of joy that came in waves and lasted for some time. So, of course, I'm wanting to recreate that. I have to remember that joy is also a state that comes and goes, so I should look at it as an experience, right?

Stephen: Yes, as you've noticed, all experiences come and go. You may experience states of joy or bliss, but they pass. Joy may be followed by sadness. Trying to hang onto the joy, or avoid the sadness is just more psychological suffering.

Q: You were so right about the possibility of doubts appearing; they come bubbling up. The doubts come in sneaky forms, I've noticed. But I remind myself that it's all mind stuff, so I just do my best to question it when it comes, and I have to say it dissipates fairly quickly.

S: Doubts come in the form of thoughts and feelings. When the doubts are questioned and seen as false, they dissipate.

Q: I think I've exhausted every way I can look at this 'I' concept. The idea that seems to really stick best with me is that if it comes and goes it cannot be what you are.

S: The real key to seeing through the 'I' concept is seeing for yourself that this 'I' that you feel you are has no power, no control over your experience. The 'I', the me, the ego, the sense of being a separate, controlling entity is false. You are not in control of what arises in awareness. You cannot hang onto the joy or avoid the sadness. Your essential nature is pure awareness. There is no 'I' that is in control.

Q: It does help to have someone to talk to. I want to tackle these doubts head on.

S: Yes, it can be helpful to talk to someone about this who can speak from personal experience.

Q: Am I really going to know for sure when it's settled?

S: When you've seen clearly that your essential nature is pure awareness, and that you are not a separate controlling ego, your spiritual search comes to an end. You'll notice that you've lost the burning desire or the all-consuming need or interest in reading spiritual books, going to seminars or retreats. Your interest in things spiritual may continue, but without the painful longing to be free. You'll feel an underlying sense of peace with whatever arises in awareness. Happiness and sadness, pleasure and pain, all come and go; but there's no resistance to what is; there's no psychological suffering.

   I call this realization Living in Peace: The Natural State. The term Living in Peace is a realistic description of your daily experience when there is no psychological suffering, no resistance to what is. The Natural State is a term that refers to your essence as awareness; awareness cannot be attained or lost, it is your eternal, Natural State. When it is realized that you are not a separate, controlling entity; and that your essential nature is awareness, you are Living in Peace: The Natural State.

Q: I think I'm still waiting for an experience of 'no-me' that is transcendental in nature, even though it's pretty darn clear there's no me. Or I'm thinking it will eventually unfold so that there is that type of experience, if I stick to the basics.

S: You may have all sorts of transcendental experiences, profound insights or epiphanies. The experiences and insights may last for a while, or they may pass quickly. You are not in control of these experiences. They come and go on their own. You cannot hold onto the pleasant experiences, or avoid the unpleasant ones.

Q: Also, I've wanted to hang on to this joy, thinking it could slip away again, as it has done so many times before. I feel pretty sure that I understand why though, I let the doubts come back in and believed them. But I'm feeling a little protective, like wanting to stick around the house or be in nature. These are all sneaky doubts, too, I guess. Whew! Kind of wears you out.

S: Yes, it is exhausting! When you realize you're not a separate, controlling entity, that there is no 'you' who can hold onto the joy, or avoid the doubts, there is quite a sense of relief. There's no one there who can grasp onto or resist whatever arises. Consciousness is all there is, and you are that. There's nothing for you to do. What a relief!

54

Fear of Letting Go of the Mind

Question: I notice there seems to be an element of panic in letting the mind drop away.

Stephen: When you say 'letting the mind drop away', what do you mean? Are you referring to losing the sense of being in control? If you feel that you are the mind, and the mind is in control, then it's understandable that a sense of panic may arise if control is given up. But is the mind in control? Are you the mind? Are you in control?

The mind is the thinking process. Thoughts arise in awareness and we call this process the mind. The mind has no independent existence, no power or control. It's merely a series of thoughts arising in awareness. So when the mind drops away, all that's happening is thoughts are dropping away. When thoughts drop away, what's left? Awareness. Awareness, your essential nature, is always here and now, always peaceful and free.

If there's a belief that you are the mind, and you are in control of your thoughts, feelings, and sensations, then it's understandable that a sense of panic is experienced when the idea of letting go of the mind arises. When it is seen clearly that you are not the mind, and the mind is not in control of anything at all, you'll experience a sense of peace and ease rather than panic when the mind drops away.

Also, you cannot let the mind drop away, nor is it necessary for thoughts to drop away to live in peace. The sense of panic drops away when it is seen that your essential nature is awareness, and the mind does not exist as a separate, controlling entity.

Q: There must be a great deal of trust that everything will be okay when I'm not directing things (apparently anyway). For example, let's take the proverbial truck on the road—if what's happening is only being registered, then why would I move out of the way? Naturally,

I've heard over and over again that the 'intelligence-energy' will deal with situations such as this as they arise, but deep down I doubt it.

S: You *are* the intelligence-energy. There is no intelligence-energy 'out there' that will take care of you 'down here'. You are that! All thoughts and actions that arise are an expression of that. The idea of trusting that intelligence-energy will take care of you implies a separation between you and intelligence-energy. You are the intelligence-energy. You don't exist as a separate entity who must trust in God, intelligence-energy, or any other such concepts.

Q: I've long since dropped the Vipassana meditation that I plunged into for years (all that noting!) But I still sit quietly and put myself in a state of deep listening. At these times I begin to understand the 'turning around and looking' aspect of this (a bad metaphor for me since I keep wanting to turn my head around like Linda Blair in the Exorcist), but panic can well up and doubts about 'doing it right' (yeah, I know, nothing to do) or even if I would recognize my true self if it revealed itself to me.

S: Your true self, or your essential nature is pure awareness, and this can be recognized right now. You are reading these words, yes? Are you aware of reading these words? Are you aware of the room you're in right now? Can you hear the noises in the background? Can you feel the chair you're sitting in? Are you aware of the thoughts that are arising in response to reading these words? Notice that awareness must be here now to register everything that arises. Without you, awareness, nothing can appear in your experience. Do you sense this presence of awareness? You *are* this awareness.

Q: I listened to your recorded radio interview with Allin Taylor, and you commented that in order for you to understand you had to make the search your own. In other words you had to see for yourself in order to take it on board.

S: The spiritual search comes to an end when you see in your own direct experience that your essential nature is pure awareness, and that you do not exist as a separate, controlling entity or ego. You can read about this for decades, but until you see this for yourself, in your own direct experience, the understanding remains conceptual. The ultimate understanding is the non-conceptual recognition that awareness is, and you are that. No words or concepts are needed.

Q: Understanding how the mind works is tricky business, and I don't think I really do understand how it works. It seems that asking the right questions can be key. Any comments?

S: It may be helpful for you to clarify what your expectations are about this understanding or realization. So, what do you want? What do you expect to get out of this? If questions or doubts come up, then you can address them. Ultimately, you'll see that the only question that needs to be answered is 'who or what am I?' and this question gets answered non-conceptually in your own direct experience.

55

Since I am Not the Body, Should I Maintain It?

Question: I have a long history of heart disease in my family. My father died at the age of fifty-two. I know that nothing can be done about the inherited genes, but the other factors that contribute to heart disease, I can have an affect on. I can eat right and exercise regularly.

Stephen: It's clear that we can't change who our parents are, and our genes are inherited from them. We had no choice in the matter—this is obvious. It's also clear that certain actions can be taken to reduce the risk of developing heart disease: eating healthy and exercising regularly.
  Some people will take action to reduce the risk of developing heart disease, and others won't. Eating healthy and exercising will either happen for you or it won't. Do you really have a choice in the matter? It's interesting to investigate the apparent process of choosing, and the sense of being a chooser.

Q: My question is, does it matter?

S: Does it matter to whom? On a relative or personal level it matters to you, your family and your friends. If you develop heart disease it matters to those to whom you're related. But on the absolute or universal level nothing is gained or lost. Galaxies, stars, planets, bodies, and cells are born, live and they die. Does the universe gain or lose anything?

Q: To borrow a phrase from the cover of *I Am That* regarding the body, *'It is not important that the body live long'*. It's difficult enough to motivate myself to exercise. It seems I always have to put aside what I've learned from the non-dual teachings, and let my ego kick in full-stride. Since I am not the body, should I continue to put effort into maintaining it?

S: Either you'll eat healthy and exercise or you won't. If effort is put into maintaining the body, it's not your effort. Effort is either happening or it's not. Is the desire and effort to exercise and eat healthy created by the ego? The ego is nothing more than the sense of being a separate, controlling entity or person. The ego is just a concept, or more accurately, a misconception. The ego has no power at all. The ego doesn't exist.

The desire and effort to exercise and maintain the body is arising from the mysterious source of all existence. The same source that created the body will either exercise it and maintain it in a healthy fashion, or let it develop disease and die. Everything that is born will one day die. On the relative or personal level it matters. But on the absolute or universal level, nothing is gained or lost.

56

Drop the Tools into the Tool Shed

Stephen: Based on your emails, it seems to me that you have a strong intellectual understanding of the pointers. You may notice that the intellectual understanding sort of sinks in to an experiential understanding—this happens on its own. As you know, everything is just happening. You'll notice that in my response to your questions below, I get the sense that you're trying to hang on to the concepts of awareness and the concepts of the absence of a separate, controlling entity. Does that seem to be the case to you?

Question: It seems the same issue is holding me up again: what I am, and what I'm not. It feels like I can only focus on one of the two key points at a time.

S: That's okay. Take a look at them one at a time.

Point one: what are you in essence? You've seen for yourself that your essential nature is awareness, yes? You're finished with point one. There's no need to focus on it anymore.

Point two: you are not a separate, controlling entity or ego. Have you seen this for yourself in your own direct experience? Have you seen that life is happening, and that you are being lived? It's not a matter of agreeing, or understanding intellectually that you have no free will, but it's a matter of seeing for yourself that there is no separate, controlling entity there in you, nor can you exercise any control over your experience. Seeing this clearly, not conceptually, but in your own direct experience, you are finished with point two. There's no need to focus on it anymore.

The two pointers are to be used as tools to help deconstruct the false sense of self. When the demolition is complete, drop off the tools. No need to focus on either of the tools any longer. Even this is just a pointer *as there is no ego to demolish and there is no one to do the demolition!* Life is happening.

Q: I can recognize that I am awareness, and that all appearances arise in that, but the recognition doesn't last long. I understand that awareness is not lost, but my identity as that awareness is forgotten by the thoughts.

S: When you say, 'the recognition that I am awareness doesn't last long', it sounds to me that you're referring to the conceptual recognition that 'I am awareness' or the thought, 'I am awareness'. Awareness is not the thought 'I am aware'. It seems like you're trying to hold onto the tools and carry them around with you at all times. That's quite a burden. Let the tools do their job and then drop them off.

Awareness is not something that can be remembered or forgotten. Thoughts, feelings, and sensations come and go in awareness, but, as you've noticed, awareness is never lost. It sounds like you're identifying yourself with the thought 'I am awareness' rather than the actual presence of awareness itself. You are not a concept. You are pure awareness itself. Do you see that awareness is not a concept?

Q: I can also look and see that in my experience there is only seeing, hearing, tasting, smelling, feeling and thinking.

S: In your own direct experience you see that there is only seeing, hearing, tasting, smelling, feeling, and thinking. The key here is that you're seeing this in your own direct experience, right? Not just conceptually, but experientially.

Q: I can see that the 'me' is only a concept that is referred to and presumed to exist. This recognition also doesn't last.

S: When you say the recognition that the 'me' is only a concept doesn't last, do you mean the thought 'the me is only a concept' doesn't last? It sounds like the understanding is conceptual, not experiential. When you see the actual absence of a me, an ego, or a separate, controlling entity in your own direct experience, you won't feel that the recognition doesn't last. There is no ego, no me that comes and goes, only thoughts come and go.

Q: In some of your correspondence, you begin by clarifying that what we are is awareness, then you move on to explain what we are not. For me, the second point seems to be more difficult and the understanding gained from the earlier pointers is sometimes lost trying to understand that there is no separate controlling entity. In other correspondence, you will not mention the second point at all. Am I supposed to be able to bear in mind that I am awareness while simultaneously looking and finding no separate self?

S: No, you can investigate the pointers one at a time. But remember they're just pointers to be used as tools. Use them, and then drop them off. If you try to hold onto the thoughts 'I am awareness, I am not the ego' you'll get frustrated and tired. A carpenter uses a hammer and saw to do his work, and then he leaves them in the tool shed when the job is done.

Q: How do these two pointers converge into one understanding?

S: When it's seen there's no ego, what's left? Awareness. This is the one, non-conceptual understanding: awareness is. Consciousness is. God is. Universal Intelligence is. The Buddha Mind is. Christ is. Is-ness is, and you are this Is-ness. There is nothing to attain and there's nothing to lose. Everything is as it is—always here and now. There is no separation.

57

I'd Like to Wake Up and Say, 'A-ha!'

Question: I have been attracted to Advaita teachings for many years since discovering the books of Wei Wu Wei some thirty-five years ago. During most of those years, I was involved with a master and yoga path that I have determined is bogus, as far as I'm concerned, and was getting me nowhere. Come to think of it, isn't that bad since Advaita teaches that there is nowhere to get to. Anyway, after all these years you'd think I'd have gotten it by now. Intellectually, I think I understand. I feel it's right under my nose like the answer to a riddle for which I've patiently waited to become clear, but now I'm tired of this.

I'd like to wake up and say 'A-ha' and be done with it. It's frustrating to feel so close to something and not have the intuitive perception of it happen. But then does it really matter if I wake up? To consciousness, I'm it whether I realize it or not. So, who cares? Since there's nothing I can do to make this happen, why bother being concerned with it? To me the most amazing thing is that there's anything at all.

Stephen: I can certainly relate to your frustration. It's extremely frustrating to feel there's a strong intellectual understanding, but there's still seeking and suffering.

From the absolute perspective of awareness, consciousness, or the universe, there are no problems. Nothing is gained or lost. But from the relative perspective of you, your family, and friends, everything matters. It's on this level that seeking and suffering happen and the problem of psychological suffering can be resolved fairly quickly and easily.

It's helpful to realize that enlightenment or awakening are just concepts and do not exist as states that can be attained. Believing in the ideas of awakening or enlightenment keep you on the path of seeking and suffering. Waiting for an 'a-ha' experience or an experience of

'I get it now' will also keep you on the path of seeking and suffering. All there is, is this. Right here, right now. This is it. There's truly nothing to get.

If you're frustrated and experiencing psychological suffering, there's an underlying belief that there's something other than what is here and now; and there's a belief that you exist as a separate, controlling entity or ego who can exercise his will to attain something better or different than what is here and now. There is no way to avoid what is here and now—happiness, sadness, anger, joy, peace or frustration. There is no way to grasp onto the pleasant experiences or avoid the unpleasant. You do not exist as a separate, controlling entity who can exercise control over your experience.

Your essential nature is pure awareness. Your essential nature has no problem with what is here and now. Your essential nature is at peace even in the midst of war. See if this is true in your own personal experience—not conceptually, but in your own direct experience. Whether you agree or disagree with all of this is irrelevant. What's important is to see and feel in your own experience that your essential nature is awareness, consciousness; and that there is no separate controller there in you who can exercise control over his life and experience.

Clearly seeing this for yourself, you may be surprised how quickly your spiritual search comes to an end, and you'll see you never had any real problems, and that everything is fine just as it is and always has been.

58

I Often Forget Who I Am

Question: I like your website and the way you communicate this, especially the point about really seeing it for oneself rather than just reading about it, which I did and it makes a difference. I do see that awareness is all I am; but I must say awareness is just another word. I think it's better to use a word that suits the mind that interprets it, if any word is worth using. For me the word 'existence' has more resonance, which is what I am, you are, and everyone is.

Do you find that since the mind is needed to understand the words you use, it depends a little on the specific mind as to how the words are interpreted? Is this why some pointers work for one person and not others?

My other question is this: I often forget who I am, especially when talking to people, or when I'm busy. I think this is because the mind gets excited, takes the view of an individual and takes over a little. Would having a reminder help, or would that simply create the problem that somebody is there to be reminded?

Stephen: It seems that finding a word or concept that strikes home for you personally is part of 'making this your own', and helps the understanding sort of sink in and move from an intellectual understanding to an experiential or non-conceptual understanding.

You said, 'I often forget who I am especially when talking to people, or when I'm busy. I think this is because the mind gets excited, takes the view of an individual and takes over a little'. Are you referring to the sense of being a separate person, an ego, a separate controlling entity seems to take over? And this sense gets triggered when you're talking with others or when you get busy, yes? This sense of being an individual, a separate ego comes and goes. We could say it's part of the human experience. It's sometimes part of the experience of being in relationship with others: family, friends, and co-workers. The ego didn't create the ego, or the sense of being a separate person; it just happens. There's no problem with it.

As you've noticed, the sense of being the ego, a separate person, just happens, and then it fades. The ego is not your essential nature, is it? Your essential nature is awareness (substitute existence—same thing), yes? That sense of being a separate ego is something that happens to you, awareness, right? Your essential nature is always awareness, even when the sense of being the ego arises in you. But the ego has no permanent, independent existence, and no power. It comes and goes. You, awareness, remain.

There's nothing that needs to be done to remove the ego from the picture, nor is there anyway the sense of being the ego can get rid of the sense of being the ego. And there's no way existence can forget that existence is existence. The sense of personal doer-ship or ego, has no separate, independent existence without existence (awareness), yes? No reminders are needed, just seeing that this is true. Existence is permanent. The ego is temporary. You are existence, not the ego.

The Burning Desire to Know Who I Am

Question: I'm at a loss. For over three years I've been reading about and listening to writings and talks about non-duality. I've been looking in my own experience for all that I've read and heard. I've read so many contradictory things: there is no one; there is no one, but the sense of 'I' remains; awakening or enlightenment is real; there is no awakening or enlightenment; you are already there; look for the 'I'.

I've spoken to non-duality teachers who say different things: one says there is no one here, and there can be a 'me-ing' to 'be-ing' flip-flop, and the other says look for your true nature, you are aware and you know you are aware and that's it! I've read so many seemingly contradictory things that I feel totally helpless. One moment the thought arises that I can do nothing, and the next moment a contradictory thought arises that I should look for the 'I' and see if I can find it. Then a thought arises that it's all just thought, and then I'm stuck. I feel like I'm being swung between looking and not looking.

Even when I do try to look for the 'I' or the sense of existence, I feel that it's all just gossamer thin mind-stuff. I have no idea what I'm supposed to be looking for. If I try to notice awareness, I doubt if it's awareness that I'm noticing and not perception. I feel like the suggestion to look for the 'I', awareness, my true nature is like trying to look for something that I've never seen while I have only a description written in terms that are so vague that I have no idea where to start, or that I would even recognize it when I come across it.

I feel that even if I don't find any presence of an 'I', I can't trust it because I just might have overlooked it. So all this makes me feel I'm stuck. Before you say that this stuck feeling just arises in awareness and has no significance, I know that. But the feeling is there, and I can't do anything about it. It comes and it goes together with the feeling that I want to get rid of it. The idea that the stuck feeling is related to the idea that I still need to get something, although intellectually, I believe there's nothing to get.

Do you see the problem? There are conflicting beliefs that keep arising and a desire to get rid of them. I don't even know who or what it is that's having these beliefs and wants to get rid of them. What I do see is that there's the belief (even this one is doubted) that once this unknown 'I' is seen to be non-existent or just seen through, the search will be over; but I have no idea what to look for.

Stephen: I can relate to the situation you find yourself in. I struggled with the same questions for years. I know what you mean about looking for the 'I', or the 'me'; or trying to find out who am I. What do I look for? I had no idea what to look for, who was looking, how I'd know if I found the 'I'. So I was terribly frustrated. The inquiry only made sense to me and became effective after I defined who or what I felt I was, in my own experience. Who does Stephen feel that he is in his gut? If I had to say who or what was the essence of Stephen, I felt that I was the controller or guide of Stephen's life. I'd heard the ego defined as the 'sense of personal doer-ship'. This made sense to me so I used that definition to look for the ego and question it. Am I in control? Am I the guide or controller of Stephen's life? Where is this controller? Does it exist? Am I the ego? What is this sense of personal doer-ship that I feel in my gut? And if I am in control then can I exercise control over my life's experience?

So you may find it helpful to ask yourself who do you feel in your gut that you are. Who do you feel you are in your own experience; not something you read in a book, how do you define yourself? When you have clarified in your own mind who you feel you are, then you can look into and question if it's true.

Q: You asked me the question what, in my gut, I feel myself to be. I really can't say, so I tried to find out, and I started with the body. Do I think or feel I am the body? Perhaps, but when I really question it, I don't think I am, because I'm willing to give that up to fulfill the desire to know what or who I am. Next, am I the mind or the thinker? No, I'm willing to give that up also. Am I the controller? This was a tricky one. But I'm willing to give that up, so I would say no. That still left me with a sense of being someone, but just someone who has given up all control, and that was where it got confusing. Because that feels like I gave up control in order to get control over knowing who I am. So it boiled down to a 'me' willing to give up control over my life, but not when it comes to knowing who or what I am. Whether I'm actually in control, I have doubts, but I sure want to be.

In the end I came to the conclusion that I seem to be the one who wants to know who he is. Being a body, a personality, or a thinker, is seen to be worthless and meaningless compared to knowing who I am. Since I seem to be willing to give up all that, I must somehow feel or think that I'm not any of those things otherwise I don't see how I'd be willing to give them up.

I left the controller out of this, because it seems to be a means to an end, an end I somehow still believe to be able to reach through that controller. Although the controller seemed more like some function I use, like I was still behind the controller. So I could see myself giving up that one, too. It seems like I'm the one wanting to know who I am.

It's like a snake biting it's own tail. That feels like a 'someone', who wants and thinks or feels he could still do something to get that, although he has no idea what or how and even doubts if it's possible at all. And in the end, I just felt like I was that one wanting to know, and also behind that. If I just say one thing I would say I feel like I'm the 'exister', the one knowing he exists, but an 'exister' wanting to know what that existing really is. In all of this there's still the feeling of being a 'someone'.

When I questioned why I wanted to know what existing really is, it seems it's because I have doubts as to whether this 'exister' or this knowing of existing, this 'I', has always been, and more importantly will continue to be? When I question why I doubt I will continue, I feel like I, the 'exister' or knower of existing, am connected to the body or mind. So that contradicts the idea I had earlier that I think that I can let go of the body/mind so I am not that body or mind.

If I leave aside all these 'why' questions, I can say that I feel like I'm the someone knowing existence, but not knowing what existing is, and wanting to find out. Am I the body/mind, the thinker, the controller? I really don't know, and I don't seem to care to be any one of them. I am knowing existence, and I want to know what that knowing is, who am I? I don't seem to be able to separate the knowing, the existing and the 'I'. Of the three, the knowing seems to be the one thing that seems most tangible. So perhaps the question, 'who am I?' is not the right question for me. Maybe the question is: 'I know that I am, I exist; what is this knowing?'

S: You wrote, 'When I questioned why I wanted to know what existing really is, it seems it's because I have doubts as to whether this 'exister' or this knowing of existing, this 'I', has always been and, more importantly, will continue to be'. What do you want or expect to get from your enquiry? It may be helpful to see what you feel your motives are. You can then question your motives to see if it is indeed possible to fulfill them. So, why are you seeking to know who you are? What do you expect will happen? What is motivating your search?

Q: By the way, thank you for corresponding with me. I feel that writing about this is already beginning to clear things up for me. I re-read what I wrote yesterday about doing the enquiry to find out whether 'I' would continue existing. This morning it seems like just a story that was fabricated out of old beliefs that no longer hold true. I don't know whether it would gain more importance again, but when I pose the 'why' question right now, all I can say is that I want to know just for the knowing. At this moment I don't even care as to whether I would continue to exist or not, I exist now, and right now there's this hunger to know and a desire to satisfy it.

The problem is that I don't know how to satisfy this hunger. As far as any expectations as to what would be left when this hunger is quenched? I have none. Well, perhaps I expect that the 'me' won't be here anymore, or the 'I' is seen through as never having been. What do I want or desire? I guess that in the end, I'd like to be free of this desire to know, and this sense of being me.

S: In your own direct experience you'll notice that at times there is a desire to know, and then the desire to know passes. The desire to know comes and goes. You've noticed this, yes? Also, in your own direct experience you'll notice that at times there is the sense of ego, or me, and then it passes, too. So, everything comes and goes—the desire to know and the sense of ego or me. Are you in control of anything that comes and goes? There's no problem with anything that comes and goes. There's no way to avoid anything that comes and goes: the sense of ego comes and goes; the desire to know comes and goes—there's no problem with any of it.

If there's anything to know, it's the fact that there's nothing to know. Existence is. Consciousness is. Awareness is. This you know non-conceptually because you are this existence, this awareness. Everything comes and goes in you, awareness, none of it is problematic. There's nothing to get, nothing to do. Everything is as it is. You are the ultimate simplicity. You are here and now. You are consciousness—period.

60

Your Will is the Will of the Universe

Question: So if there's no free will, and everything is just happening, then waking up may or may not happen, right? But then you say, 'Your seeking can come to an end'. This clearly implies that a desired goal can come to fruition. Please explain.

Stephen: Yes, it's apparent that the universe is happening. Are you in control of the universe, or is the universe in control of you? Does your will overrule the will of the universe? Is your will separate from the will of the universe? Are you separate from the universe?

My seeking came to an end when I saw there is no such thing as awakening and no such thing as being asleep. There is no one here who can wake up or fall asleep. There is no one here who can exercise his own free will. My will is the will of the universe. I am not separate from the universe. I can of my own self do nothing. I and the universe are one.

Your will is the will of the universe. Your body is the body of the universe. You are not separate from the universe. You can of your own self do nothing. You and the universe are one.

There's nothing that needs to be attained, and nothing that needs to be renounced. There's no need to go anywhere or do anything. The universe is expressing itself. Some of it you like. Some of it you don't like. It is as it is. The earth turns and the sun rises to begin a new day. All is well.

61

This is the Peace That's at Peace With War

Question: When my mind is momentarily still, all that remains is awareness. There is no concept of 'I' or anything else except what is appearing at the moment. What is appearing is not judged. It just is as it is, and it's okay whatever it is. Actually, there is not even that level of judgment. It is neither okay nor not okay. It's just happening. This awareness is expansive and encompasses all that's within it. I suppose during one of these moments I could say, 'I Am That', like Nisargadatta; but there is not even room for the thought of 'I'.

Stephen: Yes, awareness just is and you are that. There is no me, no you, no judgment, no mind. Everything is as it is. We could say you've recognized that your essential nature is awareness when this is seen. You're essential nature is non-dual.

Q: As soon as the 'I' comes back into the picture, poof, I'm back to my usual state of self-awareness, pleasure and pain, desires, frustrations, preferences, etc. (duality).

S: Yes, when the sense of 'I' comes back, there's the experience of duality: you and me; good and bad; right and wrong; pleasure and pain etc. We could say that you (awareness) are then experiencing yourself as the person, the ego, or the mind. We could say that your essential nature, which is non-dual awareness, witnesses the appearance of the person, the ego, or the mind. Awareness, your absolute, non-dual essence, experiences duality through the appearance of the person, the ego, the mind, duality.

Q: It seems to me that sages, masters, or those purported to have the understanding, maintain such a pure state of awareness in their daily lives. Perhaps I'm wrong?

S: I would say that so-called sages or masters know that their essential nature is pure awareness, consciousness, intelligence-energy, God (or whatever word works for you), and that the sense of being a separate, controlling entity is false. However, if you call the name of Jesus, or Siddhartha they would respond to you. So they also know themselves as individuals living in the world of duality. They feel pleasure and pain, happiness and sadness, and the full range of human thoughts, feelings, and sensations. It's written that Jesus, while hanging on the cross, said, 'Father, why hast thou forsaken me?' And he also said, 'I am in the world, but not of it'. So, clearly, sages experience the world of duality and all that goes with it.

Q: But it's their normal state (pure awareness) rather than an exceptional state of being for sages. For if there was not some worthwhile quality to their awareness that was sustainable, that others did not possess, there wouldn't be anything for them to write, talk about, or point to, and no one would seek them out for advice. There would be no point to satsang. Or maybe that is the point of satsang—there is no point.

S: I'd say that the so-called sage knows his essential nature is pure awareness, and that the sense of being a separate, controlling entity is temporary and false. Knowing oneself as pure awareness, not the separate person or ego, there is an acceptance of whatever arises in awareness; there is no resistance to what is. When sadness, frustration, anger, disappointment or any other so-called negative emotion arises, there is an acceptance of it as a temporary appearance, and there is no resistance to whatever arises. So we could say there is no psychological suffering, because whatever arises comes and goes freely without a fight.

Q: This is what enlightenment means to me: it's a permanent change in my way of perceiving life, from an erroneous, relative, egocentric viewpoint to something more universal and all-encompassing that provides an abiding peace, that enables me to finally say, 'Okay, that's it, I'm done. Now I see clearly there is no me to be enlightened. There was nothing to get because I was always what I was seeking and that is no thing at all. Everything is as it is and that's it'.

S: We could say that enlightenment is seeing that there is no one there who can be enlightened or unenlightened. Consciousness is all there is, and I am that. Everything is free to come and go in awareness, and awareness remains untouched, peaceful, and free. Even the sense of 'I', the ego, the sense of personal doer-ship is free to come and go in awareness. After all, the ego did not create the ego, and the ego cannot kill the ego. So it, too, comes and goes in awareness; but, it's known to be a temporary, powerless, harmless appearance in awareness, and then it fades. What's left? Awareness—always here and now. So, there's no use in fighting the ego.

Q: Am I way off here?

S: It seems to me that you were expecting that this understanding would preclude the experience of duality, or the sense of 'I', or ego. It does not preclude the experience of duality; it just puts the experience of duality into proper perspective. Happiness and sadness, pleasure and pain, the presence of ego and the absence of ego, all come and go in this non-dual presence of awareness. This non-dual presence of awareness is the Peace that's at peace with the war of duality.

62

The So-Called Sage Knows He is Powerless

Question: One of my favorite sayings is 'no resistance'. So, through no resistance to what comes up, perhaps clarity will become more constant and these old habits will become less persistent. I guess I was expecting something more dramatic and immediately life changing.

Stephen: Okay, let's have a look at this idea of 'no resistance,' and I'd also like to clarify and comment on something you said in a previous correspondence. You said, 'It seems to me that sages, masters, or those purported to have this understanding, maintain a pure, non-dual awareness in their daily lives'. Resistance, frustration, anger, sadness, the sense of ego, and the experience of duality all arise in the so-called sage, or enlightened master, just like the so-called non-sage. The difference between the so-called sage and the so-called non-sage is that the sage knows he has no power. The sage knows he cannot change what is. The sage knows he doesn't exist as a separate, controlling entity who can or must exercise his will to avoid 'negative' experiences and grasp onto 'positive' experiences. The sage is powerless, and he knows it.

Therefore, the sage merely witnesses his experience without any attempt to change it because he knows he has no power, and trying to exercise control over his experience is the *cause* of suffering, not a means to overcoming it. The so-called non-sage believes he has power to control his experience. The non-sage believes it's possible to exercise his will to avoid unpleasant experiences and grasp onto the pleasant ones. So the non-sage suffers by trying to exercise his non-existent will, generating the very suffering he's trying to avoid.

63

Going to Battle with an Unloaded Weapon

Question: The advantage, if you want to call it that, of the so-called sage is that because he knows there is no personal self that can exercise its will upon what is happening, he feels more at peace in life?

Stephen: Yes.

Q: He has a tendency toward acceptance of circumstances as they come up?

S: Yes, there's even an acceptance of rejection, and all the so-called negative emotions.

Q: He would be in this moment now, unconcerned with concepts of past and future?

S: Yes, and if he becomes concerned with the past and future there's an acceptance of that, too, and it passes.

Q: They may pass before him, so to speak, but they are observed as transient phenomena and not of any real substance?

S: Yes.

Q: And this could be described as bliss? And this bliss is expressed by the so-called sage as love, beneficence, and compassion?

S: Well, if by bliss you mean a sense of peace and acceptance, yes. Also, it may be expressed by anger or any other feeling, emotion, or thought (nothing is restricted).

Q: One thing that is often suggested is to continually question 'Who am I' and follow that to its source. This has never been very helpful to me though I think I understand what they are trying to point to. But I always end up saying 'Who am I?' and the answer is, 'I am the one who is asking the question, of course! What else!' That 'I' may not be much but it remains steadfast and I don't get past it. I do understand that the 'I' without concepts is pure formless awareness without a ripple right now.

S: Notice awareness right now. There is an awareness of the room you're in, your body sitting in the chair, you're aware of the thoughts that arise in response to the words you're reading right now. Are you aware of this awareness? Without this awareness, you couldn't see, hear, feel, or think. Do you sense the presence of this awareness that you are? It's unavoidable! It's the knowing of your own existence right now. Do you exist? <u>This sense of existence is awareness; it is your essential nature.</u> That's the first part of the answer to the question, <u>'Who am I?'</u>

<u>The second part is the realization that there is no separate, controlling entity in you who is in control of his experience. There is no one there in you who can avoid the uncomfortable feelings, thoughts, emotions; or grasp onto the pleasant ones.</u>

<u>You are awareness, not a separate controlling entity. This realization is quite a relief because you've seen that you are not in control of anything at all, so there's a surrendering that happens because you've been fighting a war all your life with an unloaded weapon! You have no power to change what is. What a relief! You can drop the question 'Who am I?' now. It has done its work. Drop off the tools at the tool shed, you're finished with the job.</u>

64

How's the Weather?

Question: The understanding seems close. In your last reply, you correctly diagnosed the remaining issue being the belief in control. The conceptual understanding had clouded my view of what I actually believed myself to be. I felt a sense of relief and excited anticipation after being honest about what I felt I was. Being honest, there is the belief that I am controlling my thoughts, my body movements and my speech, etc. It now sounds like such a meaningless statement to say that 'I' am in control. It is so obvious to me at the intellectual or conceptual level, that this 'I' is only a thought and refers to nothing real, meaning that nothing, certainly no 'one' is in control. The direct seeing of this is now the objective.

I find it difficult to stay focused on this looking for long, each time I try. Perhaps some mental discipline from meditation would have helped me here. Reading further articles or correspondence about this seems like it would possibly only complicate or conceptualize things. I do, however, wonder if there may be anything else that could help me see this clearly. Do you have any other tips at this point? I will certainly continue to investigate that 'I' that is supposed to be in control.

Stephen: If you are in control of thoughts, feelings, and sensations that arise in you, then exercise control right now. Why are you waiting? Do it now. Think only positive thoughts. Have only happy feelings. Experience only pleasurable sensations. In your own direct experience are you in control? Can you exercise control right now? Have you ever been in control in the past? Will you ever be in control in the future? Where is this separate, controlling entity that you feel yourself to be? Why are you unable to exercise control over thoughts, feelings, and sensations? Could it be that it's because there is no controlling entity there in you? Could it be the fact that life is happening?

Why do you experience psychological suffering? Because you believe you are in control of thoughts, feelings, and sensations that arise in you, and you are responsible for your experience. Are you in control of the weather? Do you control if it's raining, sleeting, snowing, cloudy or sunny outside? Why don't you experience psychological suffering when the weather is less than favorable? It's because you have no false sense of being in control of the weather. The weather is just happening. This is quite clear to you. The source of the weather is an absolute mystery. Whatever it is that is in control of the weather that arises in awareness is also in control of the thoughts, feelings, and sensations that arise. Seeing this clearly you will not experience psychological suffering over thoughts, feelings, sensations, or the weather!

Your essence is simply awareness, consciousness. You are that which is aware and conscious of all that arises in you. You do not exist as a separate, controlling entity who can exercise control over the weather, or anything else that arises in you.

The Recognition Brought On a Sense of Peace

Question: Now when I try looking for the 'I' or what I feel I am, it sets up a sense of separation. It's as if I'm looking for something else. When I first caught on to this, I stopped looking for some 'I' and started looking at myself, although I have no idea how I did this. Just like that, I recognized myself, well that's the best I can describe it. This brought on a sense of peace, and I realized that I am myself and I don't need to look for some other self or look for who or what I am. I still have no idea what this self is or how to define this or relate this to awareness, only that I am it, although at the moment 'I am it, I am myself' is just a thought and feels dead while that one instant it felt very much alive, a recognition without thought which seemed full because all feeling of wanting to know what I am was gone.

Of course, when I try looking at myself again it's difficult. Now I'm trying to look for the self I realized myself to be the first time, but I'm only able to remember some vague notion that is just the thought 'I am myself'. Somehow I don't feel it experientially like I did the first time. The first time was an experiential recognition and not a conceptual recognition that I am myself. The experiential recognition felt alive while the conceptual recognition feels dead. One needed a conceptual explanation of what I am, while the other didn't. The experiential recognition had enough on its own and nothing else was needed or wanted. Now I want this back, of course. It seems I've lost this alive recognition and what I got in return is this dead, stale thought, memory or translation of that.

Stephen: Yes, looking for what you are does set up a sense of separation. The very act of looking for oneself implies there is a self that is separate from that which is looking. You are the aliveness, the presence of awareness. You are the 'looking'. You are consciousness. You are the seeing, the hearing, the sensing, the smelling, and the tasting. You are the being-ness, the existence. Do you exist? Are you aware right now? Yes? That's it! There's nothing to find. Whatever you find cannot be you. You can only find objects arising in you. Try to avoid your own being. Try to avoid your own essence as awareness. Try to get out of the present moment. You are the non-conceptual presence of awareness. Your essence is unavoidable, indescribable, always here and now. It can never be lost.

66

Something Strange is Happening Here!

Question: I want to share with you what's been happening here. I've seen clearly that I do take myself to be a controlling entity. And I've been seeing that every time I feel this resistance and emptiness the 'doer' is always there focusing like hell, trying to make something happen. I've been asking myself, 'Do I really have the power to do anything?' I'm seeing that I haven't got much power. It seems that I'm just imagining that I'm doing things. It reminds me of Nisargadatta's statement that goes something like this, 'Stop imagining you are this or that, or you are doing this or that'. I was sitting down here just a few moments ago pondering over the sense of being the doer, the controller, or the ego.

And there came a point where there was so much space that I didn't know if I had fallen asleep or where I was or what I was. I simply was lost in being, I suppose. Something very strange is happening with me here. This spaciousness is what I am, right? Just pure being, and in this pure being there is no experience of being anybody at all.

Stephen: Your essence is pure being, awareness, and it is the witnessing presence of what is. You're noticing that your essence is just like space. Awareness has a spacious and peaceful quality with an absence of resistance. The resistance that arises is the sense of being in control of what comes into awareness. Resistance is the sense of being a separate, controlling entity, an ego. The resistance can come and go in you. You are awareness, spacious and free. Even the resistance, which is the sense of being a separate, controlling entity, is free to come and go. It is no problem. You are the spacious awareness that knows no boundaries.

You did not create the thoughts, feelings, sensations or the sense of ego. They all arise in you, spacious awareness. The world is in you. You are not in the world. Your body is in you. You are not in the body.

67

There Was a Seeing that There's Nobody Home

Question: A few days ago I was reading something written by Nisargadatta. I've read it many times before, but it never had any impact. It's something logical and easy to comprehend intellectually. It was about the fact that consciousness or the knowledge 'I am' is a product of the 'food-body' and that the body is a product of the elements (or something to that effect). In reading that, suddenly there was the seeing that there's 'nobody home'.

When I looked at my body, nobody (no-entity) was there. It seemed empty of self. Everywhere I looked everything seemed empty of self. There was no 'I' here to realize this, but the fact that 'there's nobody home' was known. If there's no 'I' in the elements, there can't be one in the body. 'I' was seen through as not existing, as something assumed. Whatever that 'I' was felt to be; the 'me' was seen to be an assumption. This sense of me or I is just that, a sense. The knowledge of existing, that's all 'I' seems to be.

I saw that since there never actually was an I-entity born that there also was no death. There's only the sense of existing that was born, and that would die, but there was nobody here to care about that. Questions about what is real, what's it all about, what is awareness and how I relate to that were seen as having no meaning since they all relate to this 'I' and there is no 'I'.

All this lasted for only a few seconds and then 'somebody' was home again. With this 'somebody' seems to come the idea that something needs to be different. There's the sense that it needs to be seen or known who I am, or that there's actually nobody here. These two seem to be the same recognition: one is positive knowledge and the other is negative.

All of this is confusing. On the one hand, it seems that recognizing myself is 'it' and that brought a sense of peace. Although I couldn't describe what I was, it did seem that I recognized myself. On the other hand, it seems that the seeing by no one that 'I' is just an assumption, and that the sense that there's nobody home is 'it'. Both seemed to give peace and both brought an end to questions, although both were only temporary.

I'm growing tired of all this chasing after experiences. So why can't I stop? Am I expecting or waiting for something to happen? Thereby chasing again after some experience that would confirm that I'm there? What is this 'there' that I want to get to? I have no idea anymore, is it recognition, knowing, peace, being? It feels that knowing who I am, finding peace, recognizing myself as awareness are worthless, just temporary nonsense appearing in whatever this typing is appearing in. No, forget that! There's nothing appearing in something else. All these things I'm chasing after are no different than typing. The one chasing is no different than the chase, the finding, the typing, or the sitting in front of this computer.

Somehow there is existing and a knowing of this existing. Even this realization feels temporary. I can feel it slipping away already, and becoming just another dead thought or memory. Do I care? It seems like I don't, but I'm just sick of chasing. Does it matter? I don't know. Who cares? How long will not caring last? I don't know. I feel like I'm at the end, ready to give in and let whatever happens happen.

Stephen: Based on our correspondence to this point, I'd say that you've seen in your own direct experience what you are *not*, and what you *are*. It's apparent to me that you've seen that the sense of being a separate, controlling entity or ego is false. You've seen and felt in your own direct experience that there's 'nobody home', as you put it. Seeing this clearly just once is enough to know with absolute certainty that the sense of I, the sense of being a separate self is false beyond doubt. Even if the sense of I comes back, you know it's just an empty, powerless appearance or sense. Your experience with this is analogous to seeing a lake in the desert that turned out to be a mirage. Initially you took the lake to be real, but upon investigation, you clearly saw that what seemed to be water was actually heat rising from the desert floor creating the false appearance of a lake. It's quite possible that the mirage may appear again, but you know it's just a false appearance.

Also, in a previous correspondence, you described your experience of recognizing that the awareness or consciousness that you were looking for as yourself, was indeed yourself, as you put it, 'I am it. I am myself'. And you described it as 'a recognition that was full because all wanting to know what I am was gone'. You also wrote that there was no way to describe what you are other than a 'knowing of existence'.

So, you've seen clearly in your own direct experience that you do not exist as a separate entity, and that what you are in essence is simply awareness or the 'knowing of existence'. Understandably, you're now feeling a sense of frustration because you feel the insights were short-lived and temporary. Don't underestimate the power of the insights you've had! We could say that the insights you've had are the beginning of the end of the false sense of self, and of psychological suffering. There's no need to struggle and fight with this anymore. Let the insights do their work. Your work is done. Everything will unfold on its own quite naturally, as it always has.

68

Nothing Mystical—Nothing Mundane

Question: I've noticed there are times after reading from your website, I may sit and do some self-inquiry and investigation. It often gives me a feeling of resistance, and then I'll go and smoke sixty cigarettes! I've also noticed many times that when I simply give up, this stuff seems to sink in automatically. Is it really like that? It either happens or it doesn't? The experience of this person is either happiness or sadness. There's really nothing I can do to accept things, to just be and enjoy the show? These thoughts have been making me very sad recently. When you discovered the falseness of the 'me', did it take some time for you to see it and let it sink in until you were convinced?

Stephen: Continuously repeating the self-inquiry and investigation will just make you tired. There's nothing you can do, there's nothing to get, nothing to discover, nothing to understand, nothing happens to you, nothing to recognize, nothing to accept, nothing to sink in, nothing to be convinced of, nothing can be avoided.

You will never be enlightened, you were never un-enlightened, there's no such thing as enlightenment, there's no such thing as being un-enlightened, there's no such thing as waking up, there's no such thing as being asleep. All there is, is this. Nothing else. There's nowhere to go, nothing to become, nothing to do. This is all there is. All there ever was is this. All there ever will be is this. There is nothing else, just this. Nothing mystical. Nothing mundane. Just this.

69

It's 4:00am: Do You Know the Source of Suffering?

Question: Our meeting has had a great impact on me, and I want you to know that. Thank you so much for taking the time.

It's four in the morning, and I'm not sleeping. I'm looking for the source of suffering. What I'm finding is that as I sit and look directly at the components of suffering they disappear. For instance, on Sunday I looked directly at this sense of control and found that not only do I not have any, but there is *no such thing!* One of the ways control liked to hide in my experience was in some unexamined belief that well, maybe I can't control *everything* that comes up, but when 'negative' stuff comes up I can do something about it, such as not express it, or say some sweet counter thought to change the energy of it.

But, excuse me, do I have any control over what appears in the first place? No! And then, by really looking at it, I saw it's just a silly idea that has no meaning and no reality. This is what I wrote that day: 'What is control anyway? I'm not finding anything that can be called control—only responses of pleasure of some kind that are then labeled control because they are liked'.

And then there's that sticky point of the body always being around. No, it's not! There is no consciousness of the body when I'm doing certain things, such as daydreaming or when I am totally focused on something I'm doing; so I am not the body. The body is in awareness. It comes and goes even in the daytime.

<u>I also looked at what makes it seem like there is a 'me' here at all, and it's only self-centered thought that makes me seem real. That *is* the 'me': self-centered thought. That's the mirage</u>. I really enjoyed your mirage metaphor and have shared it several times already and others have really benefited from it as well.

Right now, I see that belief creates my whole world. Belief creates the suffering. What is belief? Well, it's an energy that comes up and glues together with self-centered thought to create the solidity of me. The 'me' thought plus belief equals suffering! So today I'm going to keep looking straight at belief, and keep questioning it. That's what feels important to do right now. Now, one question that I have is this labeling of awareness as 'shining'. It makes me keep looking for something more than what I'm experiencing. I experience clear awareness, not shining. What is this shining description about? (And other words such as that).

Thanks for your time and I welcome any feedback and input.

Stephen: Everything you're saying feels right on to me. You are uprooting the false beliefs by examining and observing them in your own direct experience. You'll notice that all you know for certain is that you exist, consciousness is, and everything is free to come and go through you. There is no such thing as control as you noticed, just thinking, thinking, thinking.

I wrote about descriptions of awareness and the potential of them creating stumbling blocks in the correspondence entitled *Keep Asking Questions Until They're Burned Away*. Here's part of that interaction:

'There are many terms that are used to describe awareness. You've probably heard the terms emptiness and fullness. Both are correct. How can that be? Awareness is neither empty nor full. Awareness can be referred to as sparkling and light, or deep and dark. Again, both are correct, but awareness is neither light nor dark. If you've found a description of awareness that appeals to you such as: ever fresh, new, sparkling, peaceful, and you look for that description, you'll be frustrated! Awareness is, period. It is neither ordinary nor extraordinary. It just is. Anything that can be described is not awareness'.

70

Ten Days to Realize This: I Exist!

Question: Here's what's happening today: Can I find the 'I'? The 'I' is a thought arising in consciousness. Where do these thoughts come from? 'Don't know' is another thought no different from 'I'. 'Don't know' is no different from 'I' in its form or energy—it's a sensation arising in consciousness. What is aware of that? I can't find anything. I can't say what I am. There's nothing. 'I' is nothing—just a thought coming and going and telling stories about itself. All I see is a field of clear awareness and things arising in that. I can't see anything separate from that. What is awareness? Awareness is just a word that appears in clear nothing. I can't say what that is. It just is. So that's my report. I have no idea what is reporting to you. Any word I give it would just be another word.

I have been crying—why? No reason really. That would just be another story. All there is, is this clear field and what arises in it. I guess the words consciousness and awareness work for me, too. Consciousness being the stuff that comes into this clear field and names itself to itself so the play can be. Awareness is the clear field in which all arises. Wow! This is too simple for the mind that wants to figure it out. Actually, it's impossible to figure out. The mind is just thought arising in *this*. How could it ever figure it out? It's not the author. What is the author? The mind can't know. Forget it mind! How can something that doesn't even exist figure it out? All that can be known, like you and others have said, is that we exist.

And the whole ten-day thing is very funny and useful, too. Ten days to figure out that I exist. I always knew that, but in the game of hide and seek it's a useful thing to say 'I'm coming to find you now and I'm giving myself ten days!' So this unconscious postponement can come to an end.

Stephen: So many years of suffering and seeking, and then we see that at the root of the suffering there is no one there who can suffer. It was all based on a misconception of being a separate, controlling entity, a separate person, an ego who must work things out and make things right. What a relief to see there's no one there. All there is, is consciousness, this 'is-ness' that we are, and in this there is no problem. Nothing can trouble us but imagination. It was all imagination. There is nothing but *this*, here and now, and we are *this*.

71

I'm Being Moved Around Like a Puppet

Question: So, the last time I wrote there was such relief at seeing there is no one here. Then yesterday, the following day, I spent the whole day running around with my elderly parents etc., which kicked up a bunch of stuff. Let me try to get to the point here. What's being seen deeper and deeper is the control issue: that 'I' have no control. That is coming up and up and up so that it's completely seen. I woke up again in the middle of the night and was moved to the computer to read more of your correspondence and inquire and write. If I had control would I keep choosing these middle of the night episodes? Of course not. I'm just watching myself be moved around like a puppet; do this, do that. Think you're going to do something, think again, sweetie. Something else is happening now, isn't it?

I hope you can follow that; it's a description of the process occurring. Not like it's terribly different from before in some ways, but it's very different in others because the sense of any control is being stripped away and seen. Now, that's not a bad thing at all it's just not feeling complete, and that's where suffering still pops in. Of course, 'I' have no control over feeling complete. I would love to just surrender, 'Okay, control is let go of!' but as you said, and I experience, 'I' can't surrender or do any other damn thing than what is happening.

All there is, is seeing all of this, and I know that's what I am. Your pointer: 'All we know for certain is that Consciousness is, I am'. That's all that makes any sense to me. I wrote the following this morning: 'Who or what am I? This cognizing awareness makes sense at this moment. A sense of presence and what arises in it. Again, it's like the eye trying to see itself and it can't. It only sees'. So I can't see what I am; it only makes me crazy to try to do so. I can only be it, and I am it. The only thing I can 'do' is to see what is already happening: See all of this. It's nuts, I am the seeing! I do see that any suffering is just more mind stuff to be seen and not believed. Well, I've used the word 'see' a bunch of times haven't I?

If you have any feedback I, as always, would love to receive it. I feel like I have all the pointers and now the process has me. And part of it is writing to you.

I trust you know how I feel when I think of how grateful I am to you. I keep saying that but I can't help it. Your traveling all the way here initiated a very important phase here, and I feel like that lion who is ever grateful to the person who removed the thorn from its paw.

Stephen: You're seeing everything for yourself in your own direct experience. Everything is happening, but to no one. Seeing is happening. Hearing is happening. Sensing is happening. Thinking is happening. The sense of being a person with a story is happening. A sense of suffering happens. I could never find anyone here in me who was suffering. I could only find a story. The only thing I could find that seemed to be suffering was my body, and that suffering is more like an uncomfortable, bubbling energy. That uncomfortable, bubbling energy attracts attention, and then a story is developed around it. Of course, the story is all about me and my problems; me and my family; me and my... you know the story. I could never find a person who was actually suffering. There's just no one here who can suffer, only a body. It was all imagination (me and my story).

So the stories come and go. The sense of being a separate person comes and goes. The uncomfortable, bubbling energy comes and goes through the body. But there's no one to whom it's happening. Everything is just happening, to no one. I am the witnessing presence, and you are the same. <u>Nothing can trouble you but your own imagination. There's nothing to avoid, nothing to attain. There's nowhere to go, nothing to become. There is no one who can suffer. All is well.</u>

72

How Did the Suffering Return?

Question: I'll look at my experience directly as long as it takes. Actually this looking is happening much of the day. So the stories really are losing their hold; on 'no one' as you say. I resonate with your description of the uncomfortable energy as the basis for the stories. Your direct pointing brings me back home. I'm waiting for some ultimate shift to tell me that I'm always home. I see that's a trap, and yet there feels like there is some truth in that. Is there? Attention just stays with this clear aware presence when it stops running off with the stories. No one is doing that, and yet the credit still seems to be given to a 'someone' for bringing it back to awareness. That's just a subtle 'me'. It's like instead of just staying with the clarity, it just ever so slightly shifts back to a subtle thought of me. That can be seen through, too, correct?

When things shifted with you initially after visiting with John Wheeler the first time and you felt some relief, what was it like? And how did the suffering return? I ask because our minds seem to have some common ways of recreating the separate sense of the 'I' that we all share. Perhaps I could notice something going on here by hearing how that happened in your experience. And I also want to acknowledge that the sense of myself is much less dense, there is much less struggle on a daily basis.

Stephen: Initially, the suffering returned for me because I somehow had the false expectation that I should have had the 'ultimate shift', that I should have no negative emotions, that I should never drink alcohol, that I should never feel anger, etc. See how the same old stuff comes back in: the 'I should' and 'I shouldn't' thoughts? There are no shoulds or shouldn'ts. Everything is free to come and go through us. We didn't create anything that arises in awareness and we can't control what comes and goes. There may be all sorts of shifts, experiences, insights etc., but are we in control of any of them?

The subtle sense of me is free to come and go, it's just another sense or appearance arising in awareness. Trying to stay with the clear presence is another attempt to maintain control of our experience. We really have no power at all. Everything is just happening.

If there is an ultimate shift or realization, it's the realization that we can't do a damned thing about anything at all, and we never could. We are the witnessing presence. We witness war and peace; happiness and sadness; pleasure and pain; the mystical and the mundane.

Freedom from psychological suffering is the realization that we are absolutely powerless. The war with what is, is over and surrendering happens. There's no one here to put up a fight. Everything is as it is. Looking back, we see that we never had any real problems. All of our problems were imaginary and based on a false sense of being a 'me' who can exercise control: all imagination. We recognize what's real is this presence of awareness that is always here and always now. This presence of awareness that we are has no problems at all—it is always free.

73

The Pointers Found Fertile Ground

Question: Well, all of this is getting funnier and funnier. Not funny when you think *you* are at the wheel. Very funny when it's seen there's *no one* at the wheel. And how to explain that this is happening? Well, it's just like the pointers found fertile ground and are blossoming in emptiness. That sounds profound—who wrote that? But really, this process has a life of it's own now and 'I' am stepping aside and watching the show. Sometimes delusion arises, but the delusion doesn't really bite, and there's no sense of control, blame or praise. All is seen as phantom ideas occurring in aware emptiness. And once again, the ever present—Thank you!!

Stephen: Thank you for sharing your experience. I enjoy hearing from you. Well, today it's been about two weeks hasn't it? <u>It may sound odd, but it seems that two weeks is more than enough time to see in one's own direct experience that there is no separate ego here, no me, no entity with any power or control over one's life experience. Two weeks is enough time to see that life is happening now, and always has been happening. Two weeks to see that all we know for certain is that consciousness is, and the source of everything that arises in consciousness is an absolute mystery. Two weeks to see that we are absolutely powerless, and completely clueless!</u> And life goes on—it's all a mystery. So what's next? Who knows? I have no idea! Thank you for sharing your experience with this. I'm happy to correspond with you as life unfolds.

Q: Actually, I gave myself ten days, and it was on about the ninth day that the 'I' was seen through. The rest since then has been a clean up of flotsam and jetsam thrown out into awareness by habit of mind. You helped me to see through that phantom of the opera show as well. The phantom may come back and say, 'Boo', but it's just an appearance.

Looking back, I can see that when my teacher asked me, 'What if you drop all that, and tell me what's here *now?*' I looked, saw and said, 'Nothing'. It was seen then. That was in 2001 at a retreat with him. So now it's 2005 and that 'nothing' is finally really seen as all there is: nothing seeing itself as everything.

I just love your metaphor of a friend walking along the spiritual path in the desert with you and points out that the lake is just a mirage. Thank you, dear friend. Tears are welling up again. Tears of gratitude, peace, sweetness, love.

74

A Grenade Has Gone Off in the Brain!

Question: I want to share with you more strange things that are happening. Before, I felt that I was a somebody, a separate, thinking, choosing entity with power. And then some people like yourself and others pointed out that this 'me' has no power to do anything. I am aware, I see things happening, and the question arises, 'did the *me* think that thought? And, I was walking, was the *me* doing the walking? Sensations are happening, am I making them happen?' I can see it's an innocent misunderstanding that the me-image is the doer.

And now I find myself losing all interest in meetings, books, and gaining knowledge. Even the need to meditate is dropping off, almost without notice. The idea arises, 'I need to meditate, I need something', but then it passes. I have no idea what's happening, or not happening. It's like a grenade has gone off in the brain. I feel normal again and it feels good. I feel like enjoying life, partying and having fun! Oh my God, how many years have been wasted in chasing so much nonsense! To hell with the story of me! Thank you.

Stephen: Yes! Reading, meditating and all of that will not get you anywhere. If you feel like meditating, then go ahead, it's fine; but it won't give you anything more than going for a walk. If you feel like reading, then go ahead and read. You don't need to do anything to be free—you are already free. There are no real problems, just imagination. Everything comes and goes, happiness and sadness, laughter and tears, so what? It's no problem; everything passes. No one can do anything for you. You don't need anyone or anything. Everything is fine the way it is right now, right now, and right now. It's always right now. That's it, there's nothing more.

75

Why Am I Here? What's the Purpose?

Question: I was searching on the Internet and I found your website 'Living in Peace: The Natural State' and it really moved my heart. I was brought up in the Christian faith, and I've always been searching for more because nothing satisfied my hungry heart. Since my father's death seven years ago, a lot of questions have arisen in me, and I started reading about non-dualism or Advaita. I know I am more than a name; I am really the essence, the substance of the divine life, Life Itself. I know that you, my friends, my family, and me are One, even though in relative terms we can see each other as different (that is an illusion). I have intellectually accepted this last statement because it's not easy to see it; in fact, I doubt anyone has seen it.

Stephen: The mysterious Source that created the universe, the Milky Way Galaxy, and the planet we live on; the mysterious Source that makes the earth turn, the sun shine, and the rain fall; the mysterious Source that creates the birds, the fish, the plants and the animals; the mysterious Source that makes our eyes see, our ears hear, and animates our bodies; the mysterious Source that creates thoughts, feelings and sensations that arise in us; this mysterious Source is the One, it is Life Itself. Everything in existence is an appearance of the One. You are the One, I am the One, all is the One. The One appears as the many.

Q: I know, as Jesus said, that my Father and I are One, and I am pure love. What is difficult for me to understand is that apparently it does not matter if I (as awareness) love, live, or suffer. All is the same for awareness. Thus, why am I here? Maybe this is incomprehensible.

S: Does the universe have a purpose? Does our planet have a purpose? Do you have a purpose? Why is the universe here? Why is our planet here? Why are you here? Why not? It's all an absolute mystery, isn't it? Answering those questions is not necessary to live in peace. All we know for certain is that we exist, I am. Knowing yourself as I am is knowing yourself as Life Itself, the ultimate peace. There is no peace in the endless questions of the mind; there is no problem as I am.

Q: If there is not a purpose, a plan, how can I understand the suffering?

S: Is it possible to understand the purpose or plan of the universe? Is it possible to understand the plan for mankind? Do any such plans exist?

Q: For instance, a family member who suffers from a terminal disease causes terrible suffering for all family members here. How can I comfort them?

S: Take whatever action you can to help. Pain and suffering are part of the experience of life. If there are actions you can take to reduce the pain and suffering, then help in any way you can. Ultimately, it's beyond your control, but if you can help, then do so.

Q: Why did the awareness decide in each of us to assume a particular way of living?

S: It's all a mystery, is it not?

Q: Do you think the concept of the separation of mankind (in our mind) is an illusion? If it is an illusion and separation never happened, then when can I as awareness completely recover the real state?

S: Separation happens only in the mind. You are before the mind. You never lost the real state. Your essence is the real state, and you've never been separate from your own essence. Your essence is this Natural State of awareness here and now. You've always been this awareness, you are this awareness now, and you'll always be this awareness. Know yourself as this awareness, know yourself as I am—not as I was or I will be, and the illusion of separation is over.

Q: I believe in eternity. I know I am eternal life, but I suppose that, as awareness, once I leave my body I will not remember anything. So, what was the purpose of taking this body form?

S: Is there a purpose for anything at all? All I know is that I exist, consciousness is. Beyond that, I know nothing. In this 'not knowing', life happens, and there is peace with what is.

Q: Please forgive me if I am pouring all of these questions onto you and disturbing you with these crazy concerns. Thank you in advance for your kindness shown in your beautiful website.

S: I am happy to correspond with you.

76

Don't Use Any Words—Now Tell Me What's Left?

Question: I'm not having any success with the investigation into control. I feel that looking into the pointer, 'what I am', could undercut the false belief better than what fast becomes a mental investigation for me. I used to have trouble answering the simple question, 'Are you aware?' because it seems to assume there is one centralized 'you'. There are just the five main senses plus thought, which come and go. The question, 'Are you aware?' to me would mean something like 'is there perception?'

I can't find that which is unchanging and ever-present. It seems that awareness can either be like one central perceiver or it can be like the essential quality of all phenomena. Is there one, centralized awareness that perceives all the senses and thoughts? This suggests a duality of awareness and contents, a separate awareness that is aware of the senses.

Or does each individual sense arise as awareness? This would mean that there is no thing in our experience apart from the senses, no thing apart from the content. There is a quality that each phenomenon has: awareness. Without that quality, the sensation wouldn't appear. If this is correct then awareness would not be ever-present, it would only be present during the sensations or thoughts.

Stephen: Although they are the same in essence, Nisargadatta would use the term consciousness rather than awareness in your example. Using two terms helps differentiate between the absolute (awareness) and the relative (consciousness). When you are in deep sleep there is absolute awareness there, when you wake up in the morning and hear the alarm go off, there is relative consciousness. So we could say that consciousness is not ever-present, but awareness is. Awareness has no subject-object relationship. Consciousness arises with the I-thought, and the appearance of the world arises with the I-thought. What are you in essence? Awareness/Consciousness. Everything else comes and goes. You remain.

I wrote in the correspondence entitled *This Koan Called Advaita*, 'Philosophers and physicists have the pleasure (and the frustration) of attempting to describe consciousness with concepts. Some say the perceiver, the perceiving, and the perceived are one. This *one* is consciousness. Therefore, consciousness is all there is'.

All of these words are just concepts, but they point to that which you are: consciousness itself, awareness itself, life itself. Whatever word you like. There is no separation.

Q: I did not expect the scenario I presented to be correct. If each individual sense arises as awareness, with no other separate central awareness, then why can't it be said that there are six awareness(es)? Can't it be said that 'I' arise six times: seeing, hearing, feeling, tasting, smelling, and thinking?

S: Whatever we say will not be it. Consciousness is—period. Are you aware right now? That's it. Everything else is conceptual tail-chasing.

Q: Am I aware right now? I don't know what that question is asking. The only way I feel I can answer is 'there are sensations'.

S: You said, 'There are sensations'. That's it. There's nothing more. Seeing is happening through the eyes. Can the seeing see the seeing? Is the seer separate from the seeing or the seen? Consciousness is like that, too. All is consciousness. There is no separation.

No words apply. Consciousness is—period. Even consciousness is just a word. Throw away all the words and all the questions, and what's left? No words apply. That is what you are. It is inexpressible. It's analogous to trying to use words to describe the 'seeing' that's happening through the eyes. There is just seeing. How can that be described? It just is. So it is with your essence as awareness. It just is. No words apply. Do not use any words, and tell me what's left?

Words Imply Duality Where None Exists

Question: I've been at this for some time. I read J. Krishnamurti's *Commentaries On Living* around 1956. He was the first non-dualist for me. At the time, I was seeking enlightenment. He kept saying that *you* don't crave the object, but you *are the craving*; it's what you are, and that there was no 'I'. Since then, I've read most of the books on the subject; done EST twice; became a Zen Buddhist at the Rochester Zen center etc. In August this year I came across your writings and others. The idea of being already awake was a godsend. Things started making sense and are getting clearer.

My question is this: you wrote the following in the correspondence entitled *Any More Pointers?*—'Notice your own awareness. Notice your essence as awareness'. Is this not like the eye seeing itself? I'm not being picky it's just that it was pointed out to me that you cannot be aware of awareness as it makes awareness into object. It seems strange to me that I can't be aware of my awareness. Please respond if you will.

Stephen: Words imply a duality where none exists. It's the nature of language, but we don't need words to know this presence of awareness that we are. Now, I'm using words and I'm asking if you can stop for a moment, right now, and notice the fact that you are aware of these words. More accurately, there is awareness of these words, right? If we drop the words, drop the language, and sense for ourselves what the words are pointing to, we are aware, and we know it. Something is witnessing these words, something is aware of the room in which you're sitting, something is aware of the sounds you're hearing in the background, something is aware of the thoughts that are arising in response to the words you're reading now. So, there is awareness here, yes? This awareness is your essential nature, my essential nature. Without this awareness, nothing exists. The thought 'be aware of awareness' does not exist unless awareness is here to witness it. The phrase 'be aware of awareness' is just a pointer to help bring attention away from the objects of awareness and back to awareness itself. It can be a helpful pointer because it helps us realize what we are in essence, simple awareness.

Psychological suffering is caused by the misconception of being something we are not: a separate, controlling entity, and by overlooking the fact of our own existence as awareness. When it is realized that what we are is this simple presence of awareness that is aware of the seeing, hearing, feeling, thinking; and we are not a separate ego, a separate entity who has control over the objects of awareness, there is a sense of relief from the contracted experience of the ego.

So, thousands of words are written to point to that which cannot be put into words, and that which cannot be avoided: this presence of awareness that you are. Do you sense it now?

Q: Thanks so much for your reply. I have read it numerous times. So much is subtle in this, and yet when seen, is obvious.

78

Happiness and Sadness: Are They Just Energy?

Question: Thank you for giving me your time and attention tonight. It really helped, and I appreciate it very much. It was really good to talk specifically about the depression, because I kept giving it power through the label, not realizing that it's just energy that feels different from some other energy that also moves through at times.

Stephen: Yes, there seems to be a natural ebb and flow of energy through the body. When the energy flowing through the body feels light and fluffy, we label it happiness, and say that it's good. When the energy feels heavy and dull, we label it sadness, and say that it's bad. Usually a story develops around the energy and a cause-effect relationship is theorized in the mind. We must have done something wrong to cause the heavy and dull energy, and we must take action to fix it. Or we must have done something right to earn the light and fluffy energy, so let's make sure we always get it right. The stories that arise in response to the different energy patterns can become quite dramatic in the mind, but the stories are nonsense. The fact is that different energy patterns are arising through the body, there's nothing more than that. Some energy patterns are light and fluffy, others are heavy and dull.

79

The Key to Resolving Your Self-Inquiry

Question: When we're told to look and see if you can find an 'I' that exists independently, some part of my remaining ego says, 'Yes, I do exist independently. I'm in your brain. Your brain is separate, isn't it? Well, then there is a separate I, and it is you'. This is a pretty persistent little belief! It's not always like that, though. Sometimes I go looking for an independent self, and I find nothing but electrochemical impulses in a chunk of meat inside my skull. Other times I find that awareness is all, and so a sense of 'self' does not arise. Both of those are fine, but then there are those other times, when the self seems defined, self-determining, and real. So I guess you would have to say that sometimes I don't know that I am not a separate self. If I did, there would be no more need to even give it a thought!

So this seems like my next focus of inquiry, do you think? To keep asking, when I think I am a separate self, what exactly do I mean by that? When I'm feeling separate, ask myself what about me makes me separate. I don't like how it comes and goes! Why is it that I can read something like 'there is no one home in the mind' as I quoted to you tonight, and completely get it, but then later have it seem like Greek? At this very moment, I feel like there is someone home in the mind, and it's frustrating!

Stephen: Here's the key to resolving your self-inquiry. This 'I' that you sometimes feel yourself to be, this separate self that comes and goes, does it have any power to control your experience? Are you in control of your life's experience? Do you create the ebb and flow of energy through the body? Do you create the thoughts, feelings, and sensations that arise in you? Do you have any control or power over anything at all? This sense of being in control and having power to create and change our experience is at the root of psychological suffering. When you see clearly, in your own direct experience, that you have no power, no control over your experience, there is a natural surrendering to whatever is happening. Your back is against the wall, and you have no way out of what is. You are absolutely powerless. The war with what is, is over. The sense of being a separate person may come and go. After all, you didn't create it. But now you know it is powerless and harmless, and it passes just like every other appearance.

135

Q: Well, I'm going to keep working on this.

S: Another extremely important component of self-inquiry is setting a fixed time period to be finished with it. Without setting a specific time limit, it tends to be dragged on indefinitely, and the suffering continues. How many folks have been doing self-inquiry for five, ten, or twenty years? Self-inquiry is a tool. Use it and throw it away. It seems that two weeks is plenty of time to bear down and get to the bottom of this. Writing down your thoughts and experiences each day can be helpful in clarifying things for yourself, too. We may feel we have a solid understanding in our mind, but writing them down on paper helps to really clarify what's going on in your head.

Q: If you'd like to reply, please do so at your leisure. You've been very generous with your time already.

S: I am happy to share my experience with you about this. We're all floating through this life together, we might as well help each other along the way. What else can we do?

80

This Puppet Has Eyes to See and Ears to Hear

Question: I'm really applying myself to this 'finish it' project. It's good to keep focused on it because things do tend to pop through when I do.

Stephen: The earnestness and desire to be finished with the spiritual search can be an important factor in bringing the seeking to an end. The earnestness and desire arise in response to the suffering. You did not create the suffering, or the earnestness and desire to be free of it. You are the witnessing presence that is aware of it all as it unfolds.

Q: I've been journaling a lot, and I'd like to give you quick synopses as I go, so you can be on the lookout for any misunderstandings. I hope I'm not asking too much.

S: I'm happy to share everything I can with you, until you know you're finished with it. You'll know you're finished with the seeking when you realize there's no way out of the present moment. You do not create the thoughts, feelings or sensations that arise in you; they simply arise. Where do they come from, and where do they go? It's a mystery. The only thing you know for certain is that you exist. You are this existence, this sense of presence, this awareness that is always here and now witnessing the show that is written, produced and directed by the mysterious Source of all of existence. Amanda is a character in the show, and is being moved around the stage like a puppet. This puppet has eyes to see and ears to hear, but the seeing and hearing are not hers. Amanda has no power to see, hear, think, or feel— yet it's all happening. Who's doing it? Are you?

Q: So last night it was this: I got that yes, there is a brain, and yes, there is a mind, but there is no one running them. I got that there is no entity making anything happen in them. And then this morning, all the stuff that was going on in my brain was just not the least bit troubling, because it was seen as not me.

S: So you're seeing for yourself, in your own direct experience, that Amanda has no control over what arises in awareness. Where do thoughts, feelings, and sensations come from? It's an absolute mystery, isn't it? And whatever arises in awareness is just mind-stuff, it's not you, and it's not real. Nothing can trouble you but your own imagination.

Q: But it will fade in and out. It's like I get a huge realization and think, 'I'll always know this', and the next thing I know, I don't know it. I almost feel like 'I' am popping in and out of existence! I pop in, and I pop out, and I seem to have no control. Of course I have no control! That's what I just saw last night. But right now, the sense of being a separate self seems real.

S: Your real self never fades in and out. Your essence is awareness. Without awareness, there can be no sense of popping in and out of existence. What comes and goes is the sense of being a separate, controlling entity, a separate person who has power to control her experience, but you're seeing that it's not true. Thoughts, feelings, sensations, and beliefs all come and go, but you remain.

Q: Just keep doing what I'm doing?

S: You'll know when it's done. There's nothing left to do. What did you ever do anyway? Everything is happening. Everything has always been happening. Everything will continue to happen, and, in the end, nothing ever really happened. The entire spiritual search is a joke! <u>There's nothing to find, nothing to do, nowhere to go, nothing to attain, nothing to avoid, no one to do anything. All there is, is this. All there ever has been is this. This is it.</u>

81

You Can't Wake Up—You Were Never Asleep

Question: Well, I've really gotten some mileage today from the thing you wrote me about the seeing and hearing not being mine. There just keeps being no one doing anything. There keeps being nothing to do, nothing to change. There keeps being no person doing the seeing that I see. Finishing this job may come faster than I thought!

Stephen: You're seeing and realizing in your own direct experience that life is happening, but to no one. So, if no one is here *now* doing the seeing, hearing, feeling, thinking, and acting; was there *ever* anyone here doing any of it?

What is it about you that has never changed? What is it about you that is here now? What is it about you that was never asleep? What is it about you that never woke up? <u>You are awareness. You can't wake up—you were never asleep! A dream happened in which Amanda was the writer, producer, and director of her life. The dream is seen to be a dream, and it's over.</u> The dream may appear again, but now you know that a dream is a dream. There is a witnessing presence that watches all dreams, and you are that presence. It's not your presence; it's the impersonal sense of awareness that witnesses the personal experience of Amanda as her life unfolds. Everything is happening, but to no one. Consciousness is—period! There's nothing left to do, and there's no one left to do it.

—Follow up a day later—

Q: I think the end is in sight. All day long today, there has just been doing happening. What is going on is fresh, and not connected to anything else, and so there's no story that brings any emotional reaction.

One thing I think is very strange about this is that it's so bizarre that how could you ever teach this to anyone? There could never be a religion that says, 'You aren't anyone at all', because no one would join. And yet it's the only truth. It just struck me as odd that the truth is something very few people will actually believe. Once you buy into it, the rest is, I think, inevitable.

S: Nothing to buy, nothing to sell. Everything is as it is.

82

Am I in Awareness or is Awareness in Me?

Question: I'm finding your site very helpful. I'd just like to thank you for your generosity of spirit in making your understanding available to others. I hope you don't mind if I ask a couple of questions. This underlying awareness seems clear to me. I close my eyes, and it's there—vast, unfathomable and awake. It still seems localized in me, although I've read a million times that the 'me' is in it. At what point does this understanding become clear?

Stephen: There is no in or out. The 'me' is neither in awareness nor outside of awareness. The 'me' is just a thought. The word 'awareness' is just another thought. The words in and out are just thoughts. There is no separate me, no separate awareness, no in or out. They're all words, all concepts. There is no separation. Drop all the concepts, now what's left?

Q: I can rest in this awareness and a sense of awe, mystery and complete unknowing unfolds. My perception of the world becomes more luminous; there is a kind of knowing without knowing anything. I sense deeply the unity of life.

S: Yes, that's it. All there is, is awareness and you are that. You are the mystery, you are the awe, and you are the knowing that knows nothing. All is One and you are that One. Everything else is conceptual nonsense.

Q: My point is that people like you say that all this is very simple. Stop thinking and searching and there it is, no levels of understanding, just this. And I've found that to be true; but where does the knowledge or intuition come in that, for example, 'all there is, is consciousness, and consciousness doesn't arise in the brain, the brain is an appearance in consciousness, or there is nothing other than this?' How can one know for certain?

S: Is it possible to know anything at all? Every word I've said and written is conceptual nonsense. Throw it all away and what's left?

Q: I have rested in that same awareness and I know nothing. It's a complete unknowing. And then, in my case, the mind kicks in again and attempts to work things out.

S: When everything is worked out in the mind, what will you know? Not a damn thing! Having knowledge will get you a good job and good grades in school, but it won't give you the peace that you already are.

Q: All the senses are physical, and are located in this particular body. All I know of the world is dependent on the senses; all thoughts, feelings and mental states are dependent on the brain and its correct functioning. How can one know that the brain arises in awareness rather than awareness arising in the brain? At what point does this become known?

S: If your interest is to live in peace, what difference does it make if the brain is in awareness, or awareness is in the brain? There is no separation until a thought arises. Does a thought actually divide the universe into little pieces, or does a thought merely create the appearance of separation? When there is no thought, all is one. When a thought arises, does separation actually happen, does the One actually become the many; or does it just appear that way? Awareness is not in the brain, the brain is not in awareness. Nothing is separate. There is no in or out.

Q: Well, I've worn myself out again now. This constant questioning gets me nowhere, and then there will be a letting go and a resting in That. But once in that state I know nothing. Most Advaita and non-dual teachers state, with seeming certainty, that they know certain things in that unknowing, while pointing out that the awareness is the same for everyone, and there are no levels. Well, in that case why, when resting in That, do I know absolutely nothing?

S: This 'not knowing' is all there is. Everything else is conceptual nonsense. Is knowledge required for you to live in peace? Or is your seeking for knowledge disturbing the peace that you already are?

Q: I know it's the mind's thirst for knowledge that disturbs the peace that's already here, but it's a peace of complete unknowing (for the mind) which is why it gets disturbed when it reads of certain things stated by Advaita teachers, and it thinks 'well how can they really know that? I don't know that, so I must continue seeking'. It's a strange contradiction since I've followed their advice and come to the point where I know absolutely nothing. And, therefore, couldn't say from my own experience that consciousness is all there is, for example. Although the 'no self' and hence 'no free will' thing seem clear (perhaps). I'm babbling again and have confused myself. Time to switch off the mind. I look forward to hearing from you again.

S: There's no such *thing* as consciousness. Now what?

83

All Questions Dissolve in This 'Not Knowing'

Question: I've been seeking for a few years, and even though there seems to be peace at times, there are also times of intense suffering and desperation for escape. I use a series of questions that inquire into the nature of painful thoughts; but the separate entity, the one that wants something, the seeker, is still present. I often feel very frustrated that I've had some understanding of the truth, but I'm still not living it. It seems like a cruel joke to be living with this knowledge. I've tried inquiring into the 'I', but it gives me a headache, and wish I hadn't done it. I'm filled with other peoples understanding and concepts about what could happen, and my mind seems to always be there asking questions: how, what, where, when, why? Etc.

Stephen: You mentioned that at times you're experiencing intense suffering and desiring to escape. If by that you mean you're feeling suicidal, then go see a doctor immediately. There are many ways to address those feelings medically and psychologically. The concepts of Advaita or non-duality will not cure diabetes, heart disease, broken bones, hang nails, or bipolar disorder. If you're suffering from a broken leg, or clinical depression go see a doctor. If you're healthy otherwise, and would like to be free of psychological suffering, it's possible for that to happen, and I'm happy to share my experience with that.

Q: Well it's good that you picked up on the need to escape thing. I've been on prescription drugs for years, desperate to numb out my experience of reality. I do see my doctor, but I'm not sure trying new drugs is the answer for me. I feel I've fully traversed that path, but I'm open, and if it gets really bad then that's an option. Thank you for your concern.

I feel like I'm caught in a loop sometimes, even though there is a certain level of peace I still get caught up in this need to get more and to find that final answer. Each time I get caught in that loop it seems worse than before. I have only really experienced this since I started inquiring about three years ago in the sense that now I have some understanding of what is happening, I told someone that it felt like being a yo-yo.

I feel that using the series of questions that inquire into the nature of painful emotions helps me, especially when I get stuck in some painful concept. Although the teaching is from a similar non-dual perspective, i.e. there's no one doing the work, I still feel like there is someone here doing the work. After doing this for a few years my mind often hi-jacks it, and turns it into a technique rather than a natural action. Ultimately, there still seems to be someone trying to get something or get somewhere, which is why I've started this correspondence with you. I'm tired of this seeking can you help?

S: There's nothing to get. There's nowhere to go. So, can answering questions get you there? When taken to their logical conclusion, the only honest answer to all questions, including the questions who am I? What am I? Where am I? When am I? And why am I? is 'I don't know'. This sense of 'not knowing' is what you are. Everything is born, lives, and dies in this sense of not knowing. Another name for this sense of not knowing is awareness. This awareness is what you are. You can never attain this sense of not knowing, this awareness; you are it. You've always been this sense of not knowing. You'll always be this sense of not knowing. All questions are dissolved in you, this sense of not knowing.

84

Singing to the Choir: The Bullshit Song

Question: I want to be really open about what's happening here with me. I have not completely settled in with all of this. Some of the same old problems are coming back up. There is this 'me' that's looking for the uncaused joy. And I'm trying to stay with present-awareness.

Apparently, if there's any dissatisfaction, the 'me' isn't quite kicked out yet. Maybe it's the momentum of the 'me' still making itself known. Or we could say it's awakening, and not full liberation yet. We'll see.

Stephen: I know I'm singing to the choir, but all your problems are bullshit. Nothing can trouble you but your own imagination. It doesn't matter what bullshit comes back up; bullshit is bullshit. Bullshit has always been bullshit, and always will be bullshit. So what? The whole story of awakening and liberation and suffering is bullshit. Do you believe your own bullshit? I don't believe your bullshit, or my bullshit, it's all the same bullshit.

You will never wake up. You'll never be liberated. You were never asleep. It's all bullshit. Consciousness is consciousness. Imagination is imagination. Bullshit is bullshit. Flush the bullshit down the toilet, and what's left?

Q: Nothing! What a great ride! Now I'm having this subtle joy arising in the bullshit!

Who Sets the Intention to be Free of Seeking?

Question: I find your writings very helpful, especially the essay entitled *Reflections* in which you say, 'Home is awareness. Home is peace. Home is heaven. All paths to heaven lead to hell'. It was helpful when you made the suggestion to stop and look. Can you give me some pointers to look within to see who feels disturbed? Should I look at what doesn't stop, when you say, 'stop'? When I ask myself, 'What is real?' my body/mind quiets down, and feels less agitated. Should I try to look at what is real? Does that cover it?

A question that comes up for me regarding your statement that we have no control, I wonder then who is setting an intention to be free of the seeking?

Stephen: The suggestion is to investigate and see in your own direct experience who or what is in control of thoughts, feelings, sensations and actions. Are you in control? How do they arise? Did you create them? What are you in essence? Are you the ego, the guide or controller of your life? Or are you simply that which is aware of all that is? What is at the root of psychological suffering? If that root cause is seen to be false, will the suffering come to an end? These are questions that get to the root of what you are and what you are not. For me to say that you are not in control, and that what you are in essence is simply awareness, doesn't really help you.

But when you ask the questions of yourself, and look to your own direct experience for the answers, it's possible that the cause of suffering will be uprooted by simply seeing for yourself that there is no separate, controlling entity there in you, no ego, no me who has any power, and what you are in essence is simply awareness.

About your question, 'Who is setting the intention?' It's the same 'who' that's beating your heart. That 'who' is not the personal you; but the impersonal 'who' that is looking out through your eyes, and listening through your ears. Are you doing any of that, or is it just happening? Everything is happening; you are being lived.

144

86

How Does This Help Me Cope With My Life?

Question: I've been brainstorming for some days after reading your online writings and some others. I think I understand some parts. I agree that there is this unchanging awareness 24/7 and that all thoughts, experiences, feelings and sensations are functioning in this awareness. So can there be any controller here? Am I ever in control of my life? And even when I think I am, it's merely an idea. But sometimes I can't see how this can help me cope with life.

Stephen: When it is seen in your own direct experience that you do not exist as a separate ego who can exercise control over your experience, there is a natural acceptance of everything that arises. Thoughts, feelings, sensations, beliefs and actions arise in your experience, and they pass. There is no resistance to what is. Even resistance is accepted as part of the appearance, and it, too, passes. And you remain as the ever-present witness of it all.

Q: I often forget that I am not my sensations, feelings and thoughts because they appear so dominantly. For example, when someone criticizes me I get offended even though I know there's no reason to be. It's because the sensations that appear while I'm being criticized are so convincing and feel so real. What advice can you give me about this?

S: The sense of being a separate person, Gerri, arises in your experience. Sometimes Gerri is criticized, and a sense of being offended arises. Sometimes Gerri is complimented, and a sense of pride arises. Gerri, with his thoughts, feelings, memories, beliefs, preferences, and relationships is part of the play of awareness. You love Gerri and all the drama that arises in his life. You love the happiness and the sadness; the pleasure and the pain; the compliments and the criticism. Certainly you don't prefer apathy and boredom to the fresh and rich experience of being completely attached to and in love with Gerri? Do you prefer the dull and apathetic life of a stone, or the exciting life of Gerri?

Q: And another question that's been bothering me: how can there be awareness in dreamless sleep when I don't feel like I'm being aware of it? Is pure awareness even aware of it self? Is it only the consciousness in the awareness that seems to be aware that there is awareness? Therefore, can I ever have a direct experience of awareness, because I'm using the consciousness to identify it?

S: It's known that you (awareness) are there in deep sleep because if someone shakes you and says, 'wake up', you'll wake up and be conscious. What is it that registers the words, 'wake up?' Awareness registers it, and then you became conscious. There can be no direct experience of awareness because you are awareness. Seeing is happening through your eyes right now. Can the seeing directly experience the seeing? No, because the seeing is the seeing. It's the same with awareness. Awareness cannot directly experience awareness because awareness is awareness.

87

I Don't Need to Look for the Truth Anymore

Question: Well, I'm really satisfied with your answers, and I thank you deeply for them. But it's often the case that when you get an answer, more questions arise. So if you don't mind, I have a few more questions that I've been pondering lately. I always have this idea that meditation is good to see how the mind and thoughts work while you are doing nothing.

Stephen: If you find that meditating is a pleasant experience and is effective for you, then enjoy it.

Q: Is meditation necessary to awaken and avoid suffering?

S: No. Your essential nature is awareness. Awareness is already awake; you are 'awake-ness' itself. Meditating is simply another experience happening in awareness. Awareness is not affected either by sitting quietly and meditating, or jumping up and down and shouting expletives. Believing that you exist as a separate ego who must exercise his will to control his life experience is the cause of psychological suffering.

Q: I have been thinking about meditation, and I still feel that I should be meditating to avoid letting the thoughts and feelings control me.

S: We could say that your natural state is the meditative state. Your essence is the witnessing presence of all that is. So we could say that meditation, or witnessing your experience is always happening naturally. If you're meditating in an attempt to avoid or control thoughts and feelings then it will exacerbate the suffering you're trying to avoid.
   Thoughts, feelings, sensations and actions are arising in awareness. Are you creating any of them, or are they simply arising on their own? Trying to control or resist them is part of the process of psychological suffering.

Q: Why are these realized gurus telling people to meditate, when there is no one there to meditate? Zen is non-dual, but still it offers meditation. Is that really necessary?

S: If you find that meditating is a pleasant experience for you, then continue. If not, then drop it.

Q: Do you meditate at all?

S: We could say that I am the meditative state. And you are, too. But it's not a special state!

Q: How can you really say that there is absolute awareness in deep sleep? Deep sleep leaves no experience as such.

S: If you're really curious then find out for yourself; watch what happens when you go to sleep at night, and then you can answer from your own direct experience. It's an interesting question to ponder, and I've written about it, too. But it's not necessary to know that to live in peace.

Q: It is sometimes difficult to accept that I'm not this body, because that has been my belief for all my life.

S: To say that you are not the body or mind is not quite true, but awareness is your essential nature. There are times during the day that you are not aware of your body or mind, but you can never say that you are not awareness. Awareness is primary, and is your essential nature. Your body and mind are secondary, and cannot exist unless awareness is there to witness them. Verify this in your own direct experience. You don't have to believe these words, check them for yourself.

Q: Why does everything seem so real? If everything is one, why does it seem like everything is separate?

S: Everything is an appearance of the One Mysterious Source. It's the nature of thought to separate, label, and categorize. The beginning of the appearance of separation is the first thought, the I-thought. Before I am, all is one. After I am, the rest of the world of appearance is. But does thought actually divide the universe into separate pieces, or does it just appear to do so? If you want to know, check this for yourself and see what you discover.

Q: Why is my awareness in my body? If there is no body there isn't any awareness.

S: Is awareness in your body, or is your body in awareness? Does awareness have an inside or an outside, or is awareness omni-directional? Answer these questions from your own direct experience. This may be an interesting subject to meditate upon.

Q: Can there be awareness if there is not an object to be aware of?

S: Apparently, physicists agree that the seer, the seeing, and the seen are one. And we can call this 'one' consciousness. This, too, may be an interesting topic of contemplation or meditation if you feel so inclined.

Q: I'm deeply thankful for your website. It helps me a lot. I know now that I don't need to look for the truth anymore, it's always here, always present. I could especially feel it today while I was working. Whenever I was lost in thoughts, I backed up and noticed the awareness. So the thoughts kept on happening, and then they were gone. Also, I had this nice realization when I was taking a shower and I was worrying. I thought to myself, which is more real, the worries or the fact that I'm taking a shower now? And what a relief, I just let go of the feeling and worrying and I kept on showering. It's so simple.

S: Yes, you are always here and now. You can't get away from the truth of your own being; you are it. <u>Nothing can trouble you but your own imagination. All of your problems are imaginary. If you are not imagining anything, can you experience psychological suffering?</u>

Q: Still I think I need to wait a while before I can know for sure that I have understood. I have the tendency to get too excited when I discover something.

S: Consciousness is all there is, and you are that. This is it, there's nothing else.

Q: I mean, how was it for you when you realized it? How did you know that you had finally realized it?

S: I simply saw that Stephen does not exist as a separate, controlling entity who has any power to control thoughts, feelings, sensations or actions that arise. And it was obvious that all I knew for certain is that consciousness is, I am; and that this consciousness is what I am. It is the ultimate simplicity. Everything is happening, but to no one.

88

How Do You Know You're Not Already Awake?

Question: I just discovered your website and listened to your recorded radio interview with Allin Taylor. There is such a resonance with your experience of the spiritual search and finally calling off the search.

I've had several teachers with whom I have been in retreat. I've read so many books and I find a resonance with Nisargadatta as well. I'm writing because you seemed so approachable and nothing is more important to me that awakening. I woke up one day realizing I was no longer a seeker, and called off the search. Despite calling off the search there is a continued profound yearning for awakening from the illusion of a separate self.

Stephen: What was realized when the seeking stopped? Did you call off the search, or did the search somehow stop on its own? If you called off the search that day, can you call it off again now?

Q: Here's what happened when the seeking stopped: I woke up one morning and suddenly realized I wasn't a seeker. I had never identified myself as a seeker as I had yearned for Truth since I was a child. When this seeker identity fell away what was left was the question of 'Who am I?' It was very intense but not scary. There was a sudden realization that I was nothing. There were the questions of 'how do I live, how do I function in the world, what will I do for a job, who am I?' It went on and on. I was fully present yet I was a blank slate.

Of course, life continued without a hitch; I went to work, I took care of patients, I gardened, etc. It was fascinating, weird, and numbing at the same time. The numbness lasted for quite a while. That was about a year and a half ago. Much has been realized since then. On occasion there is a deep knowing of the witnessing presence.

S: So you've seen in your own direct experience that you are this witnessing presence. What is the illusion of a separate self you're referring to?

Q: I feel that intellectually there is a deep, core understanding; yet there still seems to be some sort of veil of illusion and separation that persists. It seems like it has to do with my judgment of a situation or a person's actions, etc. When this judgment arises eventually there is an awareness of judgment and then the suffering around it stops. My mind says awakening isn't here because of the judgments that continue to arise (which is itself another judgment).

S: Is the process of judgment wrong or bad? Does judgment cease upon awakening? What is the root cause of psychological suffering? Are you in control of the process of judgment? Are you in control of anything at all, or is everything simply happening?

Q: I feel so intimate yet so far away from realizing Self. There is a sense of a vacillation between awakening and illusion. I feel like instead of going the direct route, I'm taking this circuitous route to awakening, and it's very frustrating. Yet I know this is not true.

S: Can the Self be realized, or are you the Self? Are you the Self now? If not, then what are you? How will you know when you've awakened? How do you know that you're not awake right now?

Q: One thing that I think happens is that on a subtle level there is a perception that if there was Self-realization or awakening that the judgments or stories would stop as soon as they start, that I wouldn't be caught up in them.

S: What is Self-realization? Isn't it the realization that you are consciousness itself, the witnessing presence of all that is? You are not the activities of the mind, the judgments, or the stories that arise in you. The judgments and stories are not your doing, they simply appear, play themselves out, and they fade. You remain untouched. There is no need for the judgments or the stories to stop.

Q: There is a sense that I would experience life from a spacious, open perspective where there wouldn't be any resistance or attachment.

S: You are the Self, Awareness, and in you the activities of the mind take place. Resistance and attachment are activities of the mind; they come and they go. You, the Self, remain. You are the spacious openness in which the mind plays.

Q: I get caught up in stories, less so these days, but it stills happens.

S: The mind gets caught up in the stories, not you. You are the witnessing presence that watches the stories and dramas play out.

Q: There is also a perception that there would be the recognition of oneness all the time. That doesn't happen, so there is my mind's dilemma. My mind says I'm not really awake. Yet I recognize the mind can only take it to the edge of the mind and no further.

S: Stop for a moment right now. Notice the presence of awareness that is here now. Notice that it is spacious and open. Notice that these words are arising in this spacious openness right now. Notice that all of the activities of the mind, the resistance, the attachments, the stories and dramas all play out in you, this spacious, open presence of awareness. This spacious openness is what you are. This spacious openness is the Self, and you are the Self. You have always been, and always will be the Self—spacious and open.

Q: I feel like I'm a stubborn nut to crack. Sometimes I think I'm thinking too much. But then who is doing the thinking?

S: Thinking happens, but you are not the thinker. There is no problem with thinking or any of the activities of the mind. You always remain as the witnessing presence of all that arises. You are awake, you are the Self—enjoy the show!

Q: Wow! What you said above I've read and heard many times, but just now it went to the core. This stopped me:

'You are the Self, Awareness, and in you the activities of the mind take place. Resistance and attachment are activities of the mind; they come and they go. You, the Self, remain. You are the spacious openness in which the mind plays. The mind gets caught up in the stories, not you. You are the witnessing presence that watches the stories and dramas play out'.

What beautiful clarity and satsang. What I want is to always recognize consciousness consciousness-*ing*. In other words, to always be aware, or to always have that clear recognition, that I am that witnessing presence of all that arises. That is what I want. Do you know what I mean?

S: Yes, I know what you mean. Based on what you're saying it's apparent that you already know that you are the witnessing presence, you are the Self. You know this from your own direct experience.

Everywhere you go, there you are as the witnessing presence. Right now you are the witnessing presence. There is nothing mystical about your presence as awareness, you just are. There can be a tendency to spiritualize or mystify this simple presence of awareness that is always here and now, especially after having what we could call life changing experiences, realizations and insights as you've described. You are always awareness, the witnessing presence. Sometimes you witness what seem to be mystical experiences, and other times the mundane, but you are always this witnessing presence.

89

I Don't Want to Drop My Story!

Question: Many thanks for your great website. I feel there is a certain resonance and ring of truth about it. So, on to my problems! I've read some non-duality books, attended a few satsangs, and I think I have a pretty good intellectual understanding of all this stuff. I've also had the experience of pure being as the background to everything, coupled with a loosening belief in 'me'. But, here's the thing, I actually don't want to drop the story of me, with all its highs and (mostly) lows. I enjoy being justified in feeling mistreated, resentful, and bitter. Isn't that funny and sad!

Stephen: Don't you love your story? You love the drama of your life, the highs and lows, the successes and failures, the laughter and the tears. Why would you want to drop the story? Would you prefer to experience the life of a head of lettuce?

I love my own life with all of the drama, the happiness and sadness, the struggling and fighting, the winning and the losing; I love it all. I wouldn't have it any other way. It's all an incredible, unpredictable mystery. And I couldn't drop it even if I wanted to.

Q: A part of me just doesn't want to let go of this story. But why should I when all my feelings are justified? How do I go beyond this block? Should I just continue to look for the one who is attached to his story?

S: Your story is not a block, it's a fantastic movie, and you are the central character and star. Enjoy the show. Of course you're attached to your story, it's a thrilling experience, it's captivating, unpredictable, and miraculous.

Q: There's also still a feeling that I control this body, and that I am deciding when it moves and how it moves. How does one go beyond this block?

S: Feeling that you're in control of the body and mind is all part of the show. You know that you're not really in control of anything at all, but what an experience to feel that you are. It's not a block—there are no blocks.

Q: Thanks for your down to earth and practical response to my questions. I was having a bit of mental conflict thinking that I had to drop this and drop that etc. But lately there's just been a relaxing into whatever unfolds, and things are easier.

90

I Can Feel That This is Working

Question: I think my intellectual understanding of this is getting clearer. I find it strange how soon I seem to have understood it. I feel a strong sense like I'm understanding it, and knowing what it is. I feel it is non-conceptual because I don't have to think about it, I feel it all the time. I know that even though I'm not thinking of it, it's here. Is it possible to understand the fundamentals of non-duality so soon?

Stephen: How long does it take to realize that your essential nature is awareness? You stop for a moment and recognize the fact that consciousness is, and I Am That. And how long does it take to realize the fact that you do not create thoughts, feelings, sensations and actions that arise in awareness; and that you can't possibly exist as a separate ego who has power to exercise his own will? You just look and see in your own direct experience, and you've seen the fundamentals of non-duality. Consciousness is all there is, and I Am That.

Q: And is there no way to practice in order to keep this knowledge in shape? I mean is it possible to see it and then forget about the whole deal? Isn't it necessary to have some reminder to avoid going into the thoughts and the feelings?

S: Your essential nature is consciousness, and you've seen that. Thoughts and feelings arise in you, and they pass. Your essential nature remains unchanged as thoughts, feelings, and sensations come and go. This understanding is a non-conceptual understanding or seeing of these fundamental facts. No practice is necessary, just noticing or seeing the fundamentals.

Q: Would you say that this awareness is the same as The Atman, God and Tao?

S: Whatever words we use are not it. You can use whatever words you like based on your own direct experience.

Q: This awareness is not in the body? Or is it something that manifests and connects to the body?

S: Awareness is not in or out. It is omni-directional. It cannot be located.

Q: I'm getting some idea like this awareness is what gives all the living things ability to move.

S: Awareness is all there is.

Q: I'm very fond of this philosophy of non-duality. And come to think of it, I'm learning psychology, and have been very curious about how non-duality can be used for psychotherapy. I read about some people who are using the concepts of non-duality in their practice. Do you know how that goes? And does it work well? I'm very curious about that.

S: This philosophy seems to be useful and effective in all areas of living: psychology, philosophy and general daily living.

Q: I can feel that this is working; the main thing I've noticed is the boost of my confidence, that's very great. I'm also very happy about how my social skills have risen after this understanding. I think that's some sign. Also I have lost all of the intense spiritual seeking that had been causing me a lot of pain because I thought I had to act in certain ways according to some scriptures. That caused some conflicts in me.

S: Very good. Life is simple and easy when we realize that life is happening, and there is no need or benefit in fighting life as it's happening. There's the simple sense that nothing's wrong anymore.

91

Seeking a Spiritual Cure Fuels the Fire of Suffering

Question: I've been seeking for many years and I've experienced many moments of clarity followed by the usual return to suffering. In the last few years I came across non-duality and some excellent teachers. The effect has been that the separate person has largely been seen through, but still it doesn't feel quite complete. In particular I suffer from mild chronic fatigue and a general sense of ennui in my personal and professional life. Sometimes it's seen that this doesn't affect the awareness that I am, but sometimes it does seem to matter. I'm not sure if it's down to expectations that liberation should improve my health and sort out my career that keeps me in my rut. I was inspired by your determination to end the seeking and feel it's time for me to do the same. I would appreciate any advice.

Stephen: Well, the seeking came to an end for me when I saw that I couldn't do a damn thing about anything at all, and that there is no one here who can suffer. I could only watch the show. Happiness and sadness, laughter and tears—everything comes and goes and I can't do a damn thing about it, because there is no separate, controlling entity here. All there is, is consciousness, and there are no problems with consciousness.

Sometimes I feel tired, other times I have a lot of energy—that's how it is. Seeking for a spiritual cure just fuels the fire of suffering. When the seeking comes to an end, the seeking comes to an end, and here you are as you've always been; but everything is fine the way it is. If you're tired you take a nap. If you have energy you go for a walk. Nothing can trouble you but your own imagination.

Your career may get better or worse, does it really matter? Your health may improve or worsen—see a doctor if needed. Your health is what it is; it's not problematic. Nothing can trouble you but your own imagination—is this true? Right now you have no problems. All your problems are imaginary.

Q: Thank you for answering my email. It is true that the only thing that can really trouble me is my imagination, and in my case there is a switching between troubling thoughts and then pure essence, untroubled and peaceful. The same is true with seeing that there is nothing I can do about my life. Sometimes it's liberating to realize that things can only be the way they actually are, and other times there is a wishing that things were otherwise. Nevertheless, it is a relief to know that matters of health, career and personal life are actually not down to me, they just happen the way they happen. Thanks again and I will let things settle in and see how it goes.

92

Your Search is Done

Question: I've been studying non-duality rather intensively for about two years now. I've been reading web pages, books, and listening to tapes. I feel that I have a solid intellectual understanding of what is pointed to, and there have been times (few) when the seeking has stopped. But then I get doubtful, and the seeking goes on.

Stephen: What are your doubts?

Q: I think there is still some ego left that is not seen through. One of my latest discoveries was that there was a subtle believing that I was something special. I was so well cooked in that subtle belief that I overlooked it.

S: Is there a problem with the sense of ego? The belief that you are something special is the ego itself, isn't it? So if the sense of being the ego comes and goes, is it a problem? Does the ego have any real power, or does it just appear so? What are you in essence? Are you the ego, or are you awareness? The ego comes and goes. Does awareness come and go? Which one are you? Speak from your own direct experience, and what answers come up?

Q: Mostly I answer my questions myself by thinking and looking, but it would be very nice to discuss these matters with another person as I sometimes feel that I am driving in a circle.

S: Yes, it can be helpful to share your experience with another. Communicating like this helps to clarify what you know and see in your own direct experience. It helps to clear away the clouds of doubt, and to recognize that which is always present and aware.

Q: Today I have the idea that I have to be aware of awareness all the time. When or if this happens, it is done?

S: You are awareness. You can't be aware of awareness—you are it. The phrase, 'be aware of awareness' is a pointer to help bring your attention to awareness itself, and away from the objects of awareness. When it is seen that your essential nature is awareness, and that the ego is a temporary and powerless appearance in awareness, it is done. There's nothing to do. Everything is happening—to no one.

Q: Lately, much of my attention is busy with another rather compelling part of the play of life, and looking into the questions of 'what I am, and what I am not' has less attention.

S: Everywhere you go, there you are as awareness. Your attention may be focused on your family matters, your relationships, your career, or your spiritual search; but you are always there as the witnessing presence. It's not necessary to focus your attention on the questions of self-inquiry; just see that awareness is always present, and you are always That. This awareness that you are has no problems. Do you sense this presence of awareness that you are right now? Does it (you) have any problems?

Q: Some of your questions above gave rise to direct understanding: 'So it is'—and then bliss. I know that this immediate and brief understanding that was followed by a longer feeling of bliss is only an experience in awareness. When this rather rare experience happens I know I have to let it be and enjoy it.

S: So you experience peace and a feeling of bliss when you see that the sense of ego is temporary and powerless, and you recognize your essential nature is this simple presence of awareness.

Q: Yes, but soon a lot of thoughts arise such as 'Is that it? Have I taken a step more?'

S: Questions arise in this peaceful presence of awareness that you are, and appear to disturb the peace. Okay, let's answer your questions.

First, 'Is that it?' Yes, this is it. Second, 'Have I taken a step more?' No, no steps were needed. You have always been this simple presence of awareness. You can never step toward this awareness or away from it. You have always been it.

Q: Any additional comments?

S: There is no need to seek for peace or bliss. In fact, as you've noticed, the questioning and the seeking are disturbing the peace that is already here. You are the peace that you've been seeking, and you've seen this in your own direct experience. Your search is done.

93

You and Me Are the Same One: This is Love

Question: I've been reading about Advaita and non-duality. It's very clear when I read it, but in daily life it gets a bit confusing. Of course the question is always related to 'me' versus 'them'.

Stephen: Yes, of course. At the root of personal confusion, and questions in personal relationships is the belief in the existence of a separate me, a separate ego who has power to exercise his own will. If there is the unexamined belief that you exist as an independent, self-directing entity, then naturally you'll see others as independent, self-directing entities, too. Therein lies the potential for personal, egoic conflicts in relationships.

Seeing there is no separate, independent entity there in you, it is also seen there is no separate, independent entity in another. Challenges, differences and conflicts may still arise, but they are not experienced as personal conflicts. There is no personal me versus a personal you; there are just conflicts arising.

You and me are both appearances of the One Mysterious Source. If there's conflict between you and me, it's part of the play of the One. You and me are the same One in essence. Seeing you and me as the same One can be called Love.

Q: This isn't a big deal, but it gets me wondering. Should I be worried about how I behave in relationship with others? I'm always thinking that I could do better than I'm doing. I should be more giving, and say more kind words with other people. Should I contemplate this or should I just let it work out naturally?

S: It's already working itself out naturally. Everything is working itself out naturally and spontaneously. You are not the source of the kind words or of the giving. If more giving and kind words are to happen through you, you couldn't stop them. There's no separate you there to take credit for the giving or the kind words; nor to take the blame for the lack thereof. And if there's worrying about how one should behave in relationship, then there's worrying. Who can stop it? Can a volcano stop itself from erupting? Can it take any credit or blame?

Q: Sometimes when I'm talking to my father and he begins to talk over me, I sense this frustration. My body starts to shake and I begin to defend myself. But, I must admit, it has gotten better after my realization.

S: You may notice the sense that you're watching these frustrating interactions with others happen rather than being a participant in them. You are the witnessing presence of the conflict; you are not the person involved in the conflict.

Q: Does it really matter if one doesn't believe in the mind? Though I'm not choosing any thoughts I could be controlled by thoughts unconsciously.

S: Who is this 'I' that is controlled by thoughts? Isn't it just another thought? Everything is happening, no doubt, but is there an 'I' to whom it's happening?

Q: My shyness troubles me sometimes because I want to be more alive in relationship with other people. But I find myself being dull or too simple. I'm aware that this is only based on some random thoughts in my brain, but they keep circulating.

S: Some people are quiet and shy; others are loud and gregarious. Is it your doing? Is one right and the other wrong? Yes, your analysis is correct: your concerns are only based on some random thoughts circulating in you.

Q: Should I drop all my hopes of how I want to be, or should I try with ambition to be more alive in human relationship?

S: You can make an effort to be more outgoing and expressive in your relationships, but there's no need to suffer over it. If it's causing you to suffer, then drop it if you can. It's not your doing in the first place.

Q: Another example: my mother is a master at getting me worried that I'm not giving enough to other people, and that I should visit my brothers more often. But I don't feel a strong motivation to do it. Because of this, I always doubt that I understand non-duality. It's seems that sometimes I do understand, and sometimes I don't.

S: Understanding non-duality is completely unrelated to the concerns you've posed. Whether you're motivated to take certain actions, or if others are pleased with your actions, have no relation to the fact that your essential nature is awareness, and you are not the ego. Realizing this in your own direct experience, there is a sense of peace and acceptance of whatever is happening. You are the witnessing presence of all that arises. You are not the doer.

Q: This questioning of my understanding is especially apparent when I'm around people. I get shy with people that I feel are superior to me. It's a silly thought, but sometimes I don't find it effective to just drop the thought. It seems to be deeper in me than just my thoughts. There must be something deeper than transient thoughts that control me.

S: Yes, there is something infinitely deeper. In fact, so much deeper that it's an absolute mystery. The same Mysterious Source that makes the flowers bloom, the sun shine, and the earth turn is controlling this puppet called Gerri.

Q: What is it that stops me from doing whatever I want? Why do I feel shy and hesitant around some people? Why don't I express myself freely, and not worry about what others think? Maybe it's just the way my body and mind was made? Is my nature in the dual world to be shy and insecure? Or should I just let everything be as it, even if I'm shy to some people? In the end it's all just thoughts, but I've been living my life and believing those thoughts for some time. How am I supposed to drop those beliefs?

S: Is Gerri in control or is everything just happening?

Q: The fact that I am simple awareness has done more good for my mental state than any other spiritual or religious system. I now feel this deeper connection when I'm reading all sorts of spiritual writings. It feels odd that all these people are looking for something that is always in front of them.

S: Yes, stop for a moment right now and just be aware of your own existence. Do you sense this presence of awareness? There is seeing, hearing, feeling, and thinking all happening in you. No effort is required. You are this simple presence of awareness. Just stop again now and be aware. This awareness that you are can also be called Love. This Love that you are loves to laugh and it loves to cry. It loves to win and it loves to lose. It loves to be at peace and it loves to be at war. It loves to accept and it loves to reject. It loves to love and it loves to hate. This awareness that you are is unconditional Love itself. Everything that arises in it is soaked in Love. This Love is what you are.

Q: Another concern of mine is when I'm at work and I meet all these new people. Some people I find easy to speak with, and others I don't. Is it normal for a non-dualist to continue to feel uncomfortable sensations and emotions? Should I just feel them and don't think about it? Sometimes the present moment is uncomfortable. Even if I'm not consciously thinking about it, I just feel uncomfortable.

S: This puppet called Gerri along with his family, friends, and co-workers (all puppets, too) appear in your awareness. They all do their special dance, and then they part. Sometimes Gerri is comfortable and sometimes he's not. So it is.

Q: Can I be conscious of every thought I have? That just can't be. There must be some hidden thoughts and motives that keep causing me to do what I'm doing.

S: Everything in existence, including all thoughts, feelings, motives, and actions are caused by the One Mysterious Puppet Master. Gerri is a puppet, not the Puppet Master.

Q: Well, as you can see I can be a bit doubtful. This must explain why I feel an affinity to non-duality because I'm really good at seeing some flaws in other systems—be it religious or spiritual. My mind is always looking for some flaws to think about. Will my mind change if I stop worrying about it?

S: Gerri has no mind of his own. Thoughts appear and then they disappear. Where is Gerri's mind?

94

Does This Understanding Not Include God?

Question: I had always equated awakening, enlightenment, etc. with spiritual practice. I felt comfortable with that, even reassured. The last couple of years reading non-dual literature and websites, such as yours and Sailor Bob's, it feels as though I'm leaving all of that behind, and it has caused concern that maybe there is a hole where God once was, or that I never truly understood what I was referring to when I thought about God.

Stephen: What is your understanding of God? What is your understanding of yourself?

Q: I'm beginning to think that the stories were a comfort and that I have never really understood what I was looking for. Does this understanding not include God?

S: What are you looking for? When everything you have understood about God, and all of your concepts of God have fallen away, what's left? Isn't God all there ever was, all there is, and all there will ever be?

Q: It feels too late to go back now, and I hope that I'm not just looking to replace one story with another. My understanding of the principles is far from complete, but I'd appreciate a restatement of those principles.

S: The principles of non-duality can be summed up with one simple phrase, 'Consciousness is all there is, and I Am That'. What is the only truth you can speak about yourself that cannot be denied? Isn't it the fact of your own existence, the fact that you are—I Am?
And who is God?

> **Exodus 3:14,15** And God said unto Moses, I AM THAT I AM: this is my name forever, and this is my memorial unto all generations.
> **Psalms 46:10** Be still and know that I Am God.
> **John 8:12** I Am the light of the world.
> **John 14:6** I Am the way, the truth, and the life.
> **Ephesians 4:4,6** There is one body and one Spirit...One God and Father of all who is above all, and through all, and in you all.
> **John 10:30** I and my Father are One

So, now what is your understanding of God? And what is your understanding of yourself?

95

I Can't Deny That Everything is Simply Happening

Question: Regarding control: I've been calling it the 'deeply-simple level' at which it can be recognized that everything is just happening. I also think of it as the perspective of awareness, rather than the supposed perspective of the separate self. Even if I think I'm controlling a certain thought, at the most simple level it can't be denied that it is just happening. I see that everything other than that simple level is just thought about control. Any perspective or level other than awareness is just thought (me and my strange descriptions).

It was quite funny to see the thoughts rushing to catch up with all the actions, as if they're saying: 'Wait! Hey wait! I'm the one who's doing that! Slow down! And that! I'm doing that! I'm thinking that! It's me that's doing this!' The big but is that I can't stay with this recognition for more than a few seconds at a time, so it hasn't sunk into belief yet. The thoughts race in straight away, along with their built-in 'I am doing it' concept. Sometimes it's easy to recognize for another second or two, sometimes I have trouble focusing on it (due to my chatty, chaotic mind). What to do?

Stephen: Does George create thoughts, feelings, sensations, motives or actions? Yes or no? No buts, maybes or sometimes a little bit. Yes or no? What is it that witnesses the thinking and acting? Isn't it quite clear that *everything* is simply happening, and George is doing *nothing* at all? Isn't it quite clear that there is a witnessing presence that is always here and now watching everything happen?

What is George's role in this play? Is he the writer, the producer or the director of the show? Or is George a puppet-like character being moved around the stage. What is George? Is he a bundle of thoughts, feelings, sensations, memories, actions, motives, desires and fears? Is he a man, a son, a brother, a friend, a student, or an employee? Is George the creator, or a creation? What is George's essential nature? What is it about George that never changes? If there is no witnessing presence here, what happens to George?

Right now there is a witnessing presence of these words and concepts. Is this witnessing presence a concept or is it non-conceptual? Did you create this witnessing presence or is it simply happening? If this witnessing presence is not here now, can George be here now? Can anything be here now if this witnessing presence is not here to witness it?

Is this witnessing presence that you are a concept? Can this witnessing presence that you are be attained or lost? Is this witnessing presence that you are a belief? What is it that witnesses the concepts, the attainment and the loss, and the beliefs? When the chaotic mind is active, is this witnessing presence lost, or is it simply witnessing the chaos? Is this witnessing presence here for a few seconds and then gone? Can this witnessing presence be held onto? Or are these ideas just more concepts arising in this witnessing presence that is always here and now?

96

Look Away from the Stories and Let Them Be

Question: I'm still rooting out seeming vestiges of doubt. I read your correspondence entitled *Singing to the Choir: The Bullshit Song* today and enjoyed it thoroughly. I still seem to have a difficult time with the flushing of the bullshit sometimes. It seems I want to rationalize it away instead of just reaching for the lever. It's like I haven't decided whether it's just a matter of maturity to say, 'Hey, this is crap. I've seen it a thousand times before', or if I keep on digging I may get to the root of the matter and it will just stop coming up.

Of course, I'm seeing that these are just stories. So if I believe any story is true, it's a seeming move away from presence. The mind runs itself in funny circles, but it seems difficult to stop from looking to the mind for a description of what's happening.

Stephen: So you know that stories are spinning in awareness like a merry-go-round. Nothing new there, it's the same old stuff we're so familiar with. Take the focus off the stories for a while, and let them be. Notice what's watching the stories. What is the nature of this witnessing presence that watches the stories go round? What is the nature of this awareness that you are and I am? When is this awareness? Where is this awareness?

This consciousness that we are, this I am; is it love? Is it spacious, peaceful and free? Is it cold and distant, or is it warm and intimate? Does it have any boundaries or is it infinite? Can this awareness be located or is it everywhere and nowhere? Look away from the stories, and let them be. What is this awareness that we are? Is it love?

97

I'm Waiting for a Radical or Sudden Shift

Question: When one is looking for the ego or a controlling entity in oneself, and can't find it, you can't be sure that it's been overlooked. So it's effective to do what you suggest: if this controlling entity exists in you, then try to exercise control over thoughts, feelings, sensations and actions!

Stephen: Yes, if you can't find a separate ego there in you, but you still feel a sense of being in control of your experience, then go ahead and try to exercise control. Do it now. Do you create thoughts, feelings and sensations that arise, or are they just appearing in awareness? If your essential nature is not an ego, then what are you?

Q: Inspired from your comments, I'm reading Nisargadatta's *I Am That*. Nisargadatta's statement that you create the world, and that the play of life is inside you, awareness, is rather difficult for me to experience. I can understand it intellectually. As a biologist I can see that the senses receive physical and chemical stimuli, and that nerve impulses arise in consciousness—the world is created inside me. But it seems to me that I am living in the world.

S: Your essential nature is awareness; do you see this right now? You are awareness. So, does the world appear in you, or do you appear in the world? Check this right now for yourself. Don't wait for some mystical experience; just look right now and be done with this question. Everything appears in you, awareness; even the thought 'I am' appears in awareness. The Source of the 'I am', and the world is an absolute mystery; but you know you exist, or consciousness is. You are this consciousness. Without you there is no world, and no James.

Q: During a dream some months ago, I was aware that I created the content, especially the people. It was really a wonder—knowing that the scenery was created by me while I was walking through the scenery in the dream!

S: Did James create the content of the dream or did the content of the dream arise in awareness? Where is this creator of dreams called

167

James? Is he not a character in the dream, too? You are the witnessing presence of all the dreams and all the dream characters. You are not the creator of the dreams, nor are you James, the dream character. Stop and see this now. Don't wait for some experience you read about in a book.

Q: When I read your correspondence entitled *Your Search is Done* thoughts arose that I need some confirmation. I know that they are thoughts, but I still have doubts. Usually I realize doubts are just thoughts, especially the self-centered ego related ones. This didn't happen just a year ago. And now, more and more often, I recognize awareness as the now—what is. These confirmations happened gradually, so it seems to me that I am looking for a radical or sudden shift for confirmation that I've understood this, as Nisargadatta describes.

S: What is it about you that does not need any confirmation? What is it that is always here and now as you are waiting for some radical shift in perspective based on somebody else's experience you read in a book? Throw away all your books, all your thoughts, all your expectations; and when everything is gone, what's left?

98

No Separate I—No Suffering—No Awakening

Question: I need help awakening. I have several questions regarding awakening and would be thankful for your response. I have questioned myself time and again about whether there is a separate being here with any independent nature, and never find any central 'I' or anyone with control. There are just thought processes and movement of a body occurring.

Stephen: Yes, that's what this simple inquiry reveals: there is no independent, separate entity; there is no central I, there is no ego or controlling entity here. In your own direct experience all that can be found is a body and thoughts. So it's seen that there is no separate person, no independent I or ego there in you. Then what are you? What's left? What's always been here? What is it that is aware of the body and thoughts that arise? Is it consciousness? Are you this consciousness? This consciousness that you are is right here and right now.

Stop and be aware of this consciousness right now. Stop again for a moment, take a deep breath, and notice the presence of this consciousness. This is what you are. Do you notice the simplicity of this? You are this simple consciousness. This simple consciousness that you are is already awake. This simple presence of awareness that you are was never asleep. This consciousness that you are is the 'awakening' for which you've been striving. You have always been this simple presence of awareness. Without you, this consciousness, there can be no body, nor any thoughts. You are this witnessing presence that is always here and now.

Now, you've seen in your own direct experience that there is no independent I, no separate ego here; there's just a body and thoughts. So, tell me, who can awaken? Who was ever asleep? Who was suffering? There is no separate, independent person who can suffer. There is no separate, independent person who can awaken. There is only consciousness.

You are this simple presence of awareness, and in you the idea of being a separate person arose in the form of the thought 'I'. This I-thought is the birth of the appearance of separation and the beginning of personal suffering. Believing in the reality of your own existence as a separate, independent 'I', suffering is inevitable.

Seeing in your own direct experience that there is no independent I, no separate person, there can be no suffering and no awakening. The ideas of personal suffering and awakening are based on the unexamined belief in the existence of a separate I who can suffer, and a separate I who can awaken. There is no separate I.

The separate I, personal suffering, and awakening are all pure imagination. There is no I. There is no one who can suffer. There is no one who can awaken. All there is, is this consciousness, and you are this. Do you see this now? This simple recognition is the resolution of all personal suffering and seeking for awakening, liberation, and enlightenment. This is it. There's nothing to do, nothing to attain, nothing to avoid. *This is it!*

Q: In the beginning this questioning created great feelings of peace and sometimes feeling of blissful emptiness. It's been a month now since I first began. When I question my self now all I feel is stressed.

S: Drop it all. The inquiry is based on the belief in a separate I. In your own direct experience you've seen there is no separate I. It is done. The whole story of suffering and awakening falls to pieces as it was based on a false premise—an imaginary 'I'.

Q: Even though it is seen that there is no one here when the questioning occurs, when I go about my daily life it's forgotten. How is this made into a permanent realization?

S: Your daily life is happening, but there's no 'I' there who's doing it. Life is happening, but to no one. This is not a conceptual understanding that can be remembered or forgotten. It is the non-conceptual recognition that there is no independent, separate entity here; there is only consciousness. Life goes on as it always has, but for no one.

99

Is There Any Awakening or Liberation?

Question: Since I've read and heard some teachers speaking of awakening and liberation, there is still some confusion there. Some say liberation is the total fading of the 'me'. It's misleading because if you see that there is no one here but non-conceptual awareness, when the 'I' thought comes back, there is the feeling that the penny has not dropped yet, and you are back on the seeking path!

I only know one thing: I am; I exist; everything else is concepts, words, and appearances. So is there such a thing as awakening and liberation or is it a subtle way to keep seekers on the path?

Stephen: You have answered your own question beautifully! You said, 'I only know one thing: I am; I exist; the rest are concepts, words, and appearances'. Yes, that's it. The fact that you are, or I am, cannot be debated or denied. Anything that follows I am can be debated or denied: such as I am awakened, I am liberated, or I am suffering. Knowing yourself as 'I am' there is no interest in debating any concepts of awakening or liberation. Was this I am that you are ever asleep or bound? Then what was awakened? What was liberated? What was suffering?

This I am that you know so intimately is the consciousness that we all are; this simple presence of awareness. Do you sense this presence of awareness right now? This simple presence of awareness is the peace, the awakening, and the liberation that is being sought, but it's always been here! Without this simple presence of awareness there can be no concepts of suffering, awakening or liberation. This simple presence of awareness, or I am, is it. Everything else is concepts, words, and appearances. All concepts, words and appearances are free to come and go through you, and you remain as I am, untouched, always here and now.

100

That Kundalini Energy Came Up: It Scared Me!

Question: First, thank you for your visit on the phone last night. I had something very strange happen after we hung up. I felt very calm and peaceful, more so than anytime I can remember in years. Then I went to bed around 11:00pm. Now the strange part: in the middle of the night that Kundalini energy came up again. I've had it happen from time to time before, but not quite like this—it scared me. Perhaps it's because I let down all resistance, I don't know. I'm pretty shaken up over it. It's hard not to attach to a body when all that energy comes up. Any thoughts?

Stephen: The first thoughts that come to mind are about your physical well-being. If you're concerned that the energy flowing through the body may be causing physical or medical issues, you may get some relief by seeing a medical doctor to ease those concerns and address the physical effects on the body if there are any. Secondly, if you're finding that the energy is causing a mental or psychological disturbance, you may get some relief by seeing a counselor, psychologist or psychiatrist. You mentioned on the phone that you've been in contact with a therapist about this issue and the anxiety. Sharing your concerns with a professional or a specialist can provide a tremendous sense of relief, and ease your concerns.

I can speak from personal experience about the benefits of getting help from medical and psychological professionals. I found that simply sharing my experience with a medical doctor and a psychologist provided a tremendous relief from psychological suffering. You may find the same relief.

My personal experience with Kundalini energy (so-called) was brief, positive, and soothing. I had two pleasant experiences that happened essentially spontaneously. At the time, I had no previous knowledge of Kundalini. The experiences themselves were pleasant and were not problematic. However, the experiences were quite enjoyable and lasted for a couple of days each time, and, of course, I wanted the experience back again and for it to be permanent. There was some striving and struggling to reproduce the experiences over the period of several years until I gave up trying to control my experience. So there is a sense of relief that happens just by realizing I can't control my experience—the pleasant or the unpleasant.

I have no expertise or special knowledge of Kundalini, but it seems to me that while you may have no control on how and when this energy flows through your body, it is possible to be free of the psychological suffering that surrounds it.

101

The Resolution of Seeking and Suffering

Question: You asked me to look into the questions I had for myself: Is consciousness all there is in my experience, as I can verify now, or is consciousness absolutely all there is? How is the latter verified?

I wouldn't believe, for example, that this room I'm in is the only room there is, even though that is true in my current experience. I would answer that it appears that consciousness is all there is, but there are thoughts and concepts about humans, a universe, an objective reality and a brain that I accept as being true. I have no evidence that there is an external world, or that the brain is generating the sense experiences, but I choose to believe in these thoughts because they make sense, they seem rational. Solipsism is normally presumed to be the only alternative.

From the current standpoint, a private, subjective reality and an external, objective reality still seem like rational concepts in which to believe. I haven't heard a teacher explicitly say this belief is incorrect, maybe it's implied to be incorrect. That's why I hoped to get such an explicit answer from asking philosophical or theoretical questions. I can see that the idea of a subjective world and an objective world are both thoughts, but I choose to believe in these thoughts, just as I choose to believe in the existence of rooms other than the one I'm in.

So, do I need to abandon these beliefs? Perhaps I still don't truly see what's being pointed to with the word 'consciousness'.

Stephen: You are consciousness. Consciousness is. It's that simple. There's nothing else to say about it.

Q: That particular pointer just doesn't seem to be resonating, but something else has come up that seems to. I tried returning to the interpretation I had some months back. The movie analogy, which I moved away from for some reason, now seems to make a lot of sense again. Would I be on the right path or interpretation to say: 'I am this ordinary awareness, and everything else is on auto-pilot, so don't worry about it?' Is this close to the meaning or is it way off? I feel like I should stay with this for a while. The problem is that there are so many ways to interpret what teachers are saying, and I bet us seekers always leave the simplest interpretation till last!

S: You said, 'I am this ordinary awareness, and everything else is on auto-pilot, so don't worry about it'. Yes, that's it! In essence you are this simple 'witnessing presence'. Everything is on auto-pilot: the witnessing presence and all that it witnesses. Even these are concepts, but they are good pointers to what can be confirmed in your own direct experience.

Notice that this witnessing presence is always with you because it *is* you: you are this witnessing presence. Notice that everything else comes and goes, but this witnessing presence is always here and now. In your own direct experience is there ever a point in time when you can say there is no witnessing presence? Some will ask, 'What about when I'm sleeping or when I'm unconscious due to injury or medication?' There is no psychological suffering when you are unconscious or in deep sleep so the question is irrelevant to the resolution of psychological suffering.

The spiritual search and the concomitant suffering are resolved quickly and easily by seeing that nothing can trouble you but your own imagination, and that what you are in essence is this simple witnessing presence. This witnessing presence that you are and always have been is the peace that you're seeking by exercising the intellect with all of your empty and meaningless questions. The intellect has no value unless you are there to witness it!

102

Why Am I Still Seeking?

Question: I understand what I am not, and I understand what I am. I understand that seeking is a futile activity and there is nothing to seek because what I seek is what I am. I understand that and I know that. But despite knowing this I am still seeking! There is the thought 'it's stupid' because all the teachers like Sailor Bob, John Wheeler, and you constantly repeat that seeking is the disease!

What I understand right now is that there is still someone here who tries to stop seeking, and who feels puzzled about this! There is no controlling entity here who can decide to stop seeking; no shame or guilt about this—it is what it is. Questions will go on until the end. Sometimes I feel miserable to still be a seeker. When Sailor Bob says 'full stop' I would like to definitively hear him! Can you elaborate on this?

Stephen: Do you believe the bullshit story you just told? Poor Jerry is a miserable seeker, he knows the truth, but he keeps seeking. He wants the seeking to come to an end, but can't seem to stop. This is utter bullshit! All of that is just an imaginary story playing in your head. Do you see that? You are not a seeker; you are that which is watching the bullshit story playing in your head. If you believe you're a seeker today, maybe you'll believe you'll be an enlightened one tomorrow: another bullshit story! See that all stories are bullshit! You are not a seeker, and you'll never be an enlightened one.

What difference does it make whether you're watching a bullshit story about being a miserable seeker, or you're watching a bullshit story about being an awakened one? They're both bullshit stories. Meanwhile, here you are as you've always been witnessing the bullshit stories, laughing at them all. You were never a miserable seeker, and you'll never be an enlightened one. You are the witnessing presence—period.

Q: Sometimes I still believe the bullshit stories the mind tells me, sometimes not. If I had any control over thoughts, why would I choose to suffer their effects? If I had control, why would I trap myself with these bullshit stories?

S: You are not trapped at all—that's another story. And you are not suffering.

Q: So there is only a seeking game in the witnessing presence? There are just thoughts suggesting an apparent seeker? I am not the body, I am not the thoughts, and I am not the one who is presently writing this: so am I nothing?

S: You are the witnessing presence. When there is no thinking or imagining, is there any suffering? There can be no suffering without thought and imagination. You witness the thoughts and the imaginary stories. The thought 'I am suffering' and the story that follows is obviously imagination. The thought 'I am enlightened' and the story that follows are also imagination. What is real? What is not imagination? You are real, the witnessing presence. Can you suffer? Only the body can suffer, not you. All you know for certain is the fact that you are, I am. *Everything* that follows I am is not true—it is imaginary. Is this true? Do you see this now? All suffering is based on imagination. All ideas of enlightenment are based on imagination. You, the witnessing presence, are the only reality.

Q: Yes, I see that I am. There is nothing but this. All the rest is meaningless. Thank you.

103

It is Done!

Question: You're right. It is done! It doesn't matter if the ego arises; it is seen for what it is. Everything is the same, but with a relaxing into ease.

Stephen: Yes, exactly. Everything is free to come and go in awareness, even the sense of ego. Knowing yourself as the witnessing presence there is a sense of acceptance and ease with everything that arises.

Q: Sometimes when the ego arises, simultaneously there is tension in the body. Maybe when you notice tension in people it is this ego tension? And if this is true then believing in the ego is the cause of stress in people?

S: Yes, the ego is the energy of resistance to what is. When there is no resistance to what is, there is no ego and no personal stress.

Q: In my experience, seeing through the ego has happened gradually, but the search first stopped when there was recognition of myself as being, but I am not sure about this.

S: We could say that there are two key pointers that are helpful. One is to see and know what you are in essence, awareness. And, two, to see what you are not: a separate ego. This awareness that we are is the peace that we've been seeking, and the ego is the root of psychological suffering. Seeing these facts clearly is helpful to be free of psychological suffering and spiritual seeking.

Q: I'm writing this because there are a lot of thoughts about how and what to tell people about this. There is a tendency to tell people to do the same searching that I have done, but I know that there is nobody to do the searching.

S: You may find yourself sharing your experience with others. You may simply speak from the heart and share from your own direct experience. You speak what you have found to be true in your own experience.

Q: I think it's very helpful to know how it is and I think a part of the searching is this intellectual understanding. Then you are looking in the right direction and it is easier to recognize when it happens.

S: That has been my experience, too.

Q: A key part of the search is seeing through the ego that seems to happen gradually. Some of this seeing through the ego has for me been seeing how the belief in this ego character was very limiting and at the same time there must have been a recognition that this ego does not exist.

S: Seeing through the ego may happen over time for some people, and for others it may be an immediate realization that the ego is false, and all there is, is consciousness.

Q: I know there is a lot of thoughts about this and this may be an old habit of trying to understand.

S: Thoughts may continue or not. Either way, you remain as the simple witnessing presence, watching the parade of thoughts, feelings, sensations, and actions. Everything is happening to no one.

Q: Thank you, Stephen. I don't know how, but your words have been very helpful.

S: I'm happy to share my experience with this, and I am very happy there has been a benefit for you.

104

The Concept of Liberation is Another Golden Carrot

Question: The 'I' is now seen as just a thought. Some teachers say when there is a total fading of this I-thought, and that is liberation. Then liberation becomes another golden carrot (this complete fading of the I-thought). In my direct experience I can say there is more and more seeing through this 'I', and sometimes still identification with it. But even when there is the hypnosis, I know that the witnessing presence is constantly here. I know that 'consciousness is' even if there is the hypnosis or not.

These ideas of awakening and liberation were for me very misleading concepts because they imply a future time. Even to say there is only awareness is too much because awareness implies its opposite, non-awareness. Problems come from concepts. Without the concepts of time, causation, awakening, liberation, good and bad: I am, and there is no problem. Without a thought, without a story, there is just Oneness.

Stephen: Yes, well put!

105

Watching the Snow Fall

Question: First of all, thank you and all the other pointers (for a lack of a better term) for the help in clearing away doubts and conceptions that we all acquire during this sojourn of relative existence we commonly call life. It seems that after listening to Sailor Bob's Podcasts, and listening to Allin Taylor's interviews with different pointers, my experience as a seeker is almost identical with the pointers and fellow seekers.

After initial questioning and seeking in the early 70's for a meaning to life: listening to Alan Watts, reading *Be Here Now*, taking acid, etc., I passed through many esoteric teachings, but never really understood what I was seeking. About four years ago there was a realization that life had become senseless and I felt the need to recover a sincerity that had become buried under by many years of apathy, cynicism and hedonism. That urgency led once again to spirituality where meditation was again taken up. During these last few years a voracious appetite for reading and exploring all the diverse viewpoints and traditions of India coupled with sadhana has led to a receptiveness to Advaita.

During the past two weeks there has been a desire to abandon sadhana because the clarity and basic truths articulated in Advaita have left me on the edge of the void. Intuitively and experientially, true nature has been felt or seen (for lack of a better term), but it disappears very quickly. How is one to get grounded in That? Would it be possible to speak directly with you by phone?

Sincerely, watching the snow fall.

Stephen: [After a phone conversation in which we discussed That which is watching the snow fall and our relationship with That, the emails below followed.]

Q: Thanks for your time on the phone last Sunday. The conversation made everything fall into place. Now, a few days later, there is a feeling of needing reinforcement or maybe affirmation. The ego/mind thing is still lingering and pouncing from time to time. The complete, undoubted acceptance of the non-existence of this person is elusive.

Let me see if I can work this out. He who says it is elusive is just a thought arising. The emotional uncertainty arising is just an appearance in awareness. Awareness is in no way affected by thoughts or emotions. They rise and fall like waves in this sea of awareness. Wow! By doing this mini-analysis a calm has set in, and now I'm laughing at myself. I guess in my case, articulating it in this manner seems to help to fall back into awareness.

S: Yes, it is funny when you stop and notice what's really happening as you've seen yourself. Awareness is. Everything else comes and goes: thoughts, emotions, and the sense of ego. Looking out the window, I see that the snow from Sunday's blizzard has already melted; yet I am still here—watching.

I Don't Know What Awareness Is

Question: I've stopped looking for awareness in the appearance (I think). There is a sense of relaxing and sometimes a laugh at the silly actions and techniques to try to find awareness. I know what the joke of it all is going to be, but for now the silly actions and techniques will continue. I don't know exactly what awareness is. All I know is that it's not in the content. I sense that this can sometimes make awareness into another object, as if there is 'the life movie' and 'awareness'.

It's frustrating to read teachings and hear descriptions of awareness that just don't fit right now. Oneness? Space-like? Universal? Right now, it feels like I could read 'I am already the ness-ness-ness' and as long as the 'ness-ness-ness' is outside the appearance, it would have the same small effect. As long as I'm abiding as something 'back there' for a few seconds, it's like I have no positive knowledge about awareness. Or is that all this is about, getting 'me' out of the picture?

Stephen: All problems are for me. Is there any me at all?

Q: Could you tell me more about how to look for the me? Where would it be? Of course, I don't find one when I look, but I don't *not* find one either, if you know what I mean. When I look I find five senses and thoughts (though without the labels I just gave them) contained within something that I call awareness. Who looks and finds this? Thoughts. Who said that? Thoughts. Who just realized that? Thoughts. But it's not being applied. I'm answering 'thoughts', but perhaps not simultaneously seeing that was thought, too. It would be correct to think 'I am a thought' would it not? The thoughts are talking. The me is shifting as it answers these questions. So how do I fold in on myself, and stay with the questioning?

S: Does the questioner exist apart from the question, or are they one and the same?

Q: No separate questioner can be found.

S: From where are the questions coming?

Q: From nowhere

S: You are *That* nowhere.

107

Can There Be Any Mistakes?

Question: My seeking stopped just recently after discovering Sailor Bob's question: 'Can the thought 'I see' see?' Those words did something to me, and the veil was lifted. After eleven years of seeking and going down many religious paths, I couldn't believe it was so simple.

Still some questions arise, but more in the matter of can there be any mistakes since there's not a personal doer? I feel there can't be any mistakes from an absolute perspective, and definitely not from a relative perspective.

Stephen: Seeing and knowing there is no separate, personal entity in you with any personal control is the key to seeing through the ideas of personal doer-ship and of getting things right or making mistakes. Everything is happening to no one, and by no one.

As you've seen in your own direct experience, the thought 'I see' cannot see. And the thought 'I choose' cannot choose; the thought 'I am the doer' is not the doer. What is it that makes your eyes see and your heart beat? What is it that makes the sun shine and the flowers bloom? What is it that makes the dog bark and the cat purr? Is there a personal doer doing any of that or is everything simply happening?

If you're not a separate, controlling entity or ego, then what are you? What is it about you that cannot be denied? Isn't it the fact of your own existence, your own presence as the witnessing presence of all that is happening? So if you're clearly not the doer, how can there be any personal mistakes? The idea of making a mistake or getting things right applies only to a personal doer who can exercise control. There is no personal doer; there is no one with control. Consciousness is, and you are That.

108

All I Can Say Is 'I Don't Know!'

Question: I've been reading the dialogues on your website, thank you so much for sharing this knowing. Finding this non-dual philosophy just happened. I had never heard of it, and if I did, I didn't know what it was! I was looking for an explanation of why my search, my passionate and joy-filled spiritual path was ending without my permission or desire for it to end! Talk about not being in control!

This is getting deep. What is happening as I read the questions, 'Who are you, are you aware?' is simply this: 'I don't know'. It seems that all I can say about anything is I don't know! I was getting nervous, because everyone always says that it cannot be denied that I exist. Well, I don't know what that refers to? When the question is posed, 'Are you aware?' I don't know what it means? Isn't that strange? I don't know if I am aware. What do I know? *Just this!* I cannot say anymore. This, this, this, this is all I know for sure! Is this a reasonable happening in your opinion? Not-knowing awareness?

Stephen: Yes *this* is it. There's nothing else, *just this*. And your sense of 'not knowing' is exactly what is known: I don't know! It's an apparent contradiction, but what else can we say about *this*? I wrote about this 'not knowing' in the correspondence entitled *All Questions Dissolve in This Not Knowing,* and here's part of it:

'There's nothing to get. There's nowhere to go. So, can answering questions get you there? When taken to their logical conclusion, the only honest answer to all questions, including the questions, 'Who am I? What am I? Where am I? When am I? And why am I? Is I don't know'. This sense of 'not knowing' is what you are. Everything is born, lives, and dies in this sense of 'not knowing'. Another name for this sense of 'not knowing' is awareness. This awareness is what you are. You can never attain this sense of 'not knowing', this awareness; you are it. You've always been this sense of 'not knowing'. You'll always be this sense of 'not knowing'. All questions are dissolved in you, this sense of 'not knowing'.

So, what you're saying sounds right on to me.

Q: Sometimes it feels pretty strange to be in the 'I don't know' space, let alone try to communicate it to anyone else! It does seem that 'I don't know' is the only true answer. Can we ever really know anything for sure? I guess it's part of that mystery that you talk about.

I just re-read your response, and I see that you are saying that this 'not knowing' is not an *indicator* of *This*, it *is This*! 'Not knowing' is what I am (awareness)! So, I know that I don't know, and that is what I am: the unknown. Wow, that is pretty deep.

S: You can't be put into words. You are the known and the unknown. You are everything and nothing. There are no words for you.

Q: Yes, I see this. There are no words so we do our best!

I Am the Beginning and End of All Suffering

Question: I keep working with this concept of no personal doer by backtracking, so-to-speak, what led up to my decisions or actions. And each time I come up with the fact that a thought or action just came spontaneously. It just happened, and the results are what is.

Stephen: Yes, you're finding that thoughts and actions are happening spontaneously, and there is no personal doer. Right now you are seeing these words. Who is seeing these words? You can say, 'I am' seeing these words. Who or what is this 'I' that is seeing these words? Is it Paul who is seeing these words or is it simply consciousness? If Paul is seeing these words, who or what is seeing Paul? Consciousness is seeing these words, and consciousness is seeing Paul. You are consciousness.

Q: Your statement, 'Everything is happening to no one and by no one', I'm somehow not getting that. I'm alive experiencing what is. This individual experience seems to be uncomfortable and unbearable at times. There is this sense that I'm the victim of the universe and why me? I selfishly want to change things and I find out I can't. I've never controlled anything, and this is all new territory for me.

S: You said, 'I'm alive experiencing what is'. You are not alive, you are life itself. There is no separation between you and life. Life is one not two. All psychological suffering is based on a belief in being a separate entity apart from universal life itself. This separate entity is imaginary and is based on a belief that I am separate from the universe. The thought 'I am' is the beginning and end of all psychological suffering.
   There is no such thing as control. There is no separate entity in the universe. The universe is one. So who is exercising control over the universe?

Q: But through all of this, as awful as my words just stated may sound, I feel peaceful the majority of the time. So much so that those around me including my spouse and children, think I'm in a different world because I don't respond to things like I used to. There is this knowing, which is unexplainable, that it's all working out just like it's supposed to. But try explaining that to your spouse when the bills aren't getting paid, yikes!

S: Everything is happening to no one, and by no one. Can that be explained?

Q: One last question this go-round: does the knowing come that we're all one in experience and not intellectually?

S: Oneness cannot be known experientially or intellectually. There is no one to know oneness. Unity and duality are both concepts. There is no unity and there is no duality. When the thought 'I' arises, the appearance of duality arises. So, can I, over here, experience oneness over there? The thought 'I am experiencing oneness' is not oneness, it's merely another thought arising in awareness.

All there is, is this awareness here and now, and the thought 'I' arises. With the I-thought the rest of the universe appears as separate from I. But does the thought 'I' actually divide the universe into little pieces or does it just appear so? Are you the thought 'I'? Who or what sees this thought 'I'? Is the universe made of separate little pieces or does thought merely make it appear so? When there is no thought, what are you? Do you die when thought stops? Prior to thought all is and nothing is. You are all and nothing.

Q: Wow, some cobwebs are dissolving. Here are a few questions that came up. You said, 'The thought 'I am' is the beginning and end of all psychological suffering'. Could you go into that more for me? I'm confused here.

S: This simple knowing of existence, or presence of awareness can be expressed by the words 'I am'. Knowing yourself as this simple presence of awareness or I am, there is no suffering. When a story is added onto this simple presence of awareness or I am, the potential for psychological suffering arises.

For example: I am. I am Paul. I am a man. I am a poor suffering person who must take control of his miserable life and attain enlightenment. The fact of your own existence as consciousness or I am is the fundamental truth and cannot be debated or denied. But everything that follows I am can be debated or denied and is not the truth. I am the way, the truth and the life: I am, not Paul and his story.

Before there can be any suffering you must be there as consciousness, I am. Seeing that you are not Paul and his story, and knowing yourself simply as consciousness, I am, Paul and his story are seen as pure imagination and psychological suffering falls away.

Therefore, 'I am' is the beginning and end of all psychological suffering.

Q: Also, everything is happening to no one by no one. Can that be explained? No, that's a mystery to me.

S: Yes, it is a mystery. Everything is happening; is there any individual doer?

Q: You said, 'Prior to thought all is and nothing is. You are all and nothing'. Are the words all and nothing just pointers to pure awareness?

S: Yes, awareness is everything in absolute terms, and nothing in relative terms. Awareness is what is seeing these words right now. You are awareness, not Paul. Nothing can trouble you but imagination. Stop and notice your own existence as awareness. Just stop and notice it now. I AM.

110

I Can't Get Past the Sense That I Am This Body/Brain

Question: You know, I think I get it, and then more doubts arise. The recurrent doubt is about being the body/brain. Why can't I get away from this? I listen to your audios and read what you write, and I hear what others are saying and writing, but I just keep screwing it up or missing the point.

Stephen: Here's the point: you are consciousness. Everything else comes and goes through you. Everything that comes and goes is temporary and irrelevant. You are always here and now. Stay with what you know. Stay with the fact that you exist, I am. Everything else is absolutely irrelevant to this understanding and living in peace here and now.

Q: It's a bit embarrassing. How can I ever get past this sense that I am the body/brain? It seems that without this body/brain, you and I couldn't be having this conversation, right? The thoughts seem to be arising in this brain. It's not that I can feel them, but the thoughts seem to be in this head. Without the brain in this head we wouldn't be having this conversation. So, how can I not be the body/brain?

S: You said, 'It seems that without this body/brain, you and I couldn't be having this conversation, right? So, how can I not be the body/brain?' Yes, that's true. But why stop there? Without water, oxygen, or energy from the sun, we wouldn't be having this conversation either. How can you not be water, oxygen, or energy from the sun?

You are the oxygen, carbon, hydrogen, nitrogen, and calcium that make up the body and brain. You are the protons, neutrons, and electrons (and the space between them) that make up the atoms. You are the atoms that make up the molecules. You are the elements that make up the body and brain. You are not just a body with a brain; you are everything and nothing.

Q: I understand that I could remove a foot or leg or arm or more and still be me, but remove the brain and I wouldn't be conscious for this conversation. You could even, theoretically, remove my heart and replace it with a mechanical pump and I would still be here. But my brain seems a totally different story.

S: If we remove one atom of hydrogen from all of the water molecules in your body and brain, you won't be conscious either, in fact the body would not exist at all. So are you just an atom of hydrogen?

Q: While I understand that the brain is not self-powering, that there has to be a life essence that powers the brain, it seems that it takes the brain for the life essence to know itself, to be conscious of itself, of life. How can I know that it is not the brain that is itself conscious of the thoughts it produces?

S: Stay with the simplicity of what you *do* know. You know there is consciousness, I am. Do you need a degree in biology, chemistry, psychology, or metaphysics to know that you exist? The teaching of non-duality is the ultimate simplicity. All is one and you are that. You are that which is witnessing these words right now and you are the words. There is nothing that you are not. You are the simple presence of awareness that you know in your own direct experience that is always here and now.

You are life itself. You are everything and nothing. You cannot be put into words or taken apart into little pieces. You are not a concept. You are not just a body and a brain. You are not just an atom of hydrogen. You are all and nothing.

Q: When I had a surgical procedure a few years ago and was under a general anesthetic, everything disappeared because the consciousness centers of the brain were, in essence, put to sleep. The brain kept working so the body would function, but there was no consciousness/awareness of anything.

S: <u>That experience reveals the fact that consciousness is essential to all experience. Consciousness is primary; experience is secondary.</u>

Q: I have a very hard time with this and would like to be as certain as you and others. If your answer is to investigate, while this might sound stupid, please tell me how. Maybe I've been doing it wrong all these years. It is embarrassing that others get this and teach it to others and seem to have such a different experience afterwards and yet I keep limping along, missing it every time. I would like to be done with this and know it with certainty, but instead I read another book or download another talk. Please help me see what I am missing about this.

S: You are consciousness, I am: stay with that. Everything else is imagination and is irrelevant. It's that simple. Don't complicate it with empty and meaningless doubts and questions. Stay with what you know. Stay with what cannot be questioned, debated or denied. Stop right now and sense this presence of awareness. Just stop now. Notice this simple witnessing presence. Here and now there is awareness of these words—you are this awareness. Everything else is conceptual nonsense. It *is* this simple.

111

I AM: Everything Else is Imagination

Question: Indeed the suffering does end when I stop and simply see myself as awareness. You explained the beginning and end of all psychological suffering so clearly for me. [see the correspondence entitled *I Am the Beginning and End of All Suffering*] I can relate it to a quote from Revelation: I am Alpha and Omega, the beginning and the end.

The questions that come up after this knowing seem so insignificant because I can stop and notice I am, and there's peace. Is this the peace talked about in the midst of the storm? This whole story of life is more like a dream: pictures keep changing, but I don't, and that makes it more funny than fearful to me.

Stephen: Yes, this is the Peace that surpasses all understanding. This is the Peace that's at peace with war. This is the acceptance that accepts rejection. This is the Love that loves hate. This I Am. Everything else is imagination.

112

I Feel Like an Alien

Question: I have some questions here. I know I am consciousness, that's an obvious fact. But sometimes I find myself thinking too much about it, and trying to convince other people about it. I don't know why I do this. Maybe it's still just a concept for me: being consciousness.

Stephen: There's no need to talk to anyone about non-duality. Personally, I talk only to people who approach me about it. Life is happening quite naturally. Awareness is expressing itself as the play of life. The sense of ego that many people experience is part of the play, and can be enjoyable for you to play along.

No need to convince anyone of anything at all. If someone approaches you and asks a question, you simply speak from your heart and your own direct experience. You speak what you have found to be true yourself. There's no interest in convincing anyone of anything at all.

Q: This sometimes leads to moments when I think I haven't understood the pointers (or better said, seen where the pointers are pointing). And since that time I haven't been any more peaceful. I feel like my reactions to myself and the environment should have changed after the realization. And now, since I'm so into this non-duality stuff, I find myself complicating my life more than ever before. It seems that everything can be misused—even non-duality pointers.

S: Yes, throw away all the pointers and live from your heart. No need to bother yourself or anyone else with all these non-duality concepts.

Q: I find so many contradictions when I see my self as consciousness because everybody else sees them self as a person, and, therefore, I feel like an alien. I find it hard to understand other people's opinions because I feel like having no opinion is the thing.

Also there are so many people who are always talking about bad things, rambling and complaining; that makes me totally empty for conversation. And even as I'm saying this to you, I see the nonsense of it all. I still believe the thoughts. And I find it really difficult to quit believing. Do you have any advice for me?

S: You know that the thoughts and beliefs of others, and the thoughts and beliefs that arise in you are just an appearance. Opinions, beliefs, rambling thoughts and complaints are all part of the play of life. No need to do anything at all with them. Everything is fine the way it is. Nothing touches you. You merely watch the play of life as it unfolds. You are love itself, loving all that comes into your experience. There's nothing to do or say—just be as you are. There are no real problems.

It Really is This Simple, Isn't It!?

Question: Okay, suddenly (or not so suddenly!) it is clear that this seeing-knowing-witnessing has always been here, and absolutely everything else has changed. This body, these thoughts, emotions, sensations; all of them arise out of nowhere and pass away into nowhere and always have—always have!

Memory (which is seen as just another arising in this moment) shows that this consciousness is what has never left. It saw childhood, high school, grandparents, prior worries and desires. All of those appearances (I get the term 'appearances' now—they really are just temporary) have come and gone. But the *seeing* of them is the same now as always. Even this note, these thoughts that create this note, arise and are the seeing, the consciousness.

Your pointing out that the person 'Vernon' is another arising in imagination really hit home. Vernon is just another idea; another construct in imagination, but that which sees Vernon is that which I am. The thoughts and imagination continues; maybe it always will, maybe not. Who knows or cares? It really doesn't matter, does it? It only matters when the fiction is believed. The movie is only scary when it is forgotten to be a movie.

Even happiness arises in this. But the arising, whatever it might be, no matter how beautiful or misshapen, still arises only in this space, this consciousness. So this idea of clarity may come and go, but it still comes and goes in the awareness. In the end, nothing can obscure the awareness, including the idea that awareness is obscured!

I've seen the thoughts come and go in just these few days since we spoke. And it's clear that it is only thought that creates psychological suffering. I see it happening again and again. But the *seeing* is not at all impacted by the seen. So anything can come up in the space; it's only thinking interfering with other thinking that creates discomfort. Kind of like two different wave patterns colliding with each other to create a chaotic pattern or static, yet nothing needs to be done about it. More doing is like adding another wave to the pattern or trying to get the snow globe to clear up by shaking it harder!

Well, this is all a little weird, probably, that I would write this to you. I'm just writing because it just really hit me. It kind of snuck up on me after our talk, and I wanted to share what now seems so clear.

You know, this whole 'end of psychological suffering' thing is a big deal. Thinking, conceptualizing, and imagination really is the source of all upset, and it really is completely tied to how the 'problem' impacts 'me'. What is so clear now is that the 'me' really is just an arising in awareness, too. Because there is *seeing* the thoughts which construct the problem as well as *seeing* the idea of 'me' that the thoughts are interfering with. Again, two wave patterns interfering with one another.

Well, I hope this makes some sense. I really appreciate your willingness to talk to me about all this. And, for all I know, I'll be calling you in a week! However, I've got to tell you, this seems very obvious right now, and it seems that there is no way to escape the seeing, you know? There may well be more confusion that arises in the form of thought (questioning, conceptualizing, etc.), but the seeing is still taking it all in. It really is this simple, isn't it.

Stephen: I read your email through twice. Everything you said is absolutely right on. You're seeing in your own direct experience that you *are* the seeing, the knowing, the witnessing of everything that arises. You are consciousness itself, I am.

You're seeing that Vernon and his story are simply appearances in you. You're seeing that psychological suffering is nothing more than thought, imagination, and a belief in the existence of a central character called Vernon. You're seeing that you are this witnessing presence of all that arises, and that nothing can trouble you but imagination.

You're seeing that you have always been this simple presence of awareness, and will always be. Now you know yourself as I am, and nothing can trouble you. All sorts of stories and experiences are free to come and go through you, and you remain untouched as this simple witnessing presence. No thought, no doubt, no story, no experience can ever touch you. You are the witnessing presence of everything that appears in you.

You're seeing everything clearly. There's nothing more to do, nothing to attain, nothing to avoid. Yes, it is this simple.

Waiting for the Explosive Moment of Realization

Question: I've been listening to some of your audio clips on your website and found them to be very helpful. I think I'm quite lucky as I have only been seeking for a couple of years (I'm only twenty-one), albeit very intensely, and feel the search is resolving. I feel very connected with simple presence at the moment, and I'm able to catch my self-centered thoughts quite early, and thus loosen their grip. However, although I believe and conceptually understand the absence of any independent entity, and know all life to be the present awareness that I am, I still cannot completely see this.

Stephen: Your essential nature is consciousness. No belief, concept, or understanding is required to know that you exist, I am. Without consciousness, nothing else exists for you.

Q: I haven't had an explosive moment where 'I' vanished, although I feel the truth of it often.

S: <u>You may have many interesting experiences or explosive moments, and then they'll pass. What's left is what's always been here, this simple presence of awareness that you are.</u>

Q: What do you suggest happens now? Is it simply a matter of keeping presence a conscious experience, and watching thoughts in order to catch the ego out, hoping that a final realization will one day happen?

S: The final realization is that there is no final realization and that nothing needs to happen or be done. You are this witnessing presence, and this witnessing is already happening. You have always been this witnessing presence. Everywhere you go, there you are as this witnessing presence. You are the simple presence of awareness that is aware of these words right now. In a few moments something new will come into awareness, but awareness remains. You are always this simple presence of awareness. No effort is required. Awareness just is, and you are this.

Q: Although I can feel that I am no thing other than presence, I worry that I will lose myself in thoughts again soon. I'm still waiting for the over-the-edge moment when my ego is seen to have not been there, but for this to last forever.

S: <u>You cannot lose yourself. In fact, try to lose or get away from awareness. It's not possible. Thoughts and feelings of being lost arise, and you witness them. You are this witnessing presence. You cannot be attained or lost.</u>

115

Give it up and Go Wash the Dishes

Question: I'm having doubts about the existence of this awareness, and I hear this is a common occurrence during the search. If there is no me, then there is no me to have a true nature. Isn't the sense of being presence-awareness still a feeling of self? I am told that this is just the paradox that is solved when you see what is being pointed to.

Okay, but there can never be an experience of awareness, it just gets defined as something that is there and that I already am. I could say that I have looked for months now and here are the results: there is no self-entity, just thoughts about one. There are sensations, thoughts and feelings and that is absolutely all.

These things are not appearing in something—that would be conceptual. They are not appearing on something—that would be conceptual. They exist, and they seem to be self-perceiving as what we call sensations. Still, though, I feel like a separate entity, and it remains an intellectual observation. Bearing in mind the rarity of seekers ending their search, there is the desire to get to the bottom of this particular doubt.

Stephen: What is it that cannot be doubted?

Q: The bare sensations and thoughts that are before critical thinking and doubt.

S: Look at this from your own direct experience. Who is aware of the sensations, thoughts and doubts? In your own direct experience you can say, 'I am'. In your own direct experience you can say, 'I am aware of sensations, thoughts, doubts, and my spiritual search'.

Who is reading these words? I am. Who is aware of sensations? I am. Who is aware of thoughts? I am. Who is aware of the body? I am. Who is seeking answers? I am. Who is having doubts? I am. Who is thinking? I am. Who is the common denominator in all your experiences? I am. Who is always here regardless of what's being experienced? I am. I am with you always—I am. I am this simple presence of awareness. Everything else comes and goes, but always, I am here and now.

Q: I would not answer with 'I am' if I wanted to answer correctly. 'I am' is a thought, and any other experience to do with the words 'I am' is another sensation, feeling or thought. Who is aware of the sensations? Nobody. If I put anything there as being aware of the sensations, that is a concept. Surely that 'I am' is just a thought and perhaps an associated feeling.

S: The word 'apple' is not an apple. The words 'I am' are not the I am. Who is aware of these words? I am. Not the thought. The word apple has no nutritional value. But the apple itself is quite nutritional. The words 'I am' are not aware. You are aware. Who is aware? I am.

Q: There is no who, no me or I. I am not the thought 'I am' nor any sense of 'I am', no identity at all. It seems to me that whatever the words 'I am' represent, whatever they are pointing to, will be a sensation, a feeling or some sense of self. All there is direct evidence of is sensations. This is the doubt that there is an awareness that 'I am'.

S: Who knows that?

Q: The one who knows that is the mind.

S: Who knows the mind?

Q: The knowledge or belief comes through the thoughts. Couldn't thought, by definition, appear without the need for awareness?

S: Appear to whom?

Q: This is not my experience right now as I still feel myself to be a separate entity, as if I was trapped feeling that the sky is literally blue.

S: Who is feeling oneself to be a separate entity? Nisargadatta suggests staying with this sense of awareness or 'I Am'. I suggest you do the same. It's apparent that using the intellect to discover that which is aware of the intellect is a fruitless method. Give it up. Stay with this sense of presence. Meditate on it, ponder it, and know it. Find out about this sense of presence, I am. Drop everything else. It's much too simple for your advanced intellect. I AM—stay with that. Everything else is a waste of your time.

Q: Thought does not need to appear to a person or an 'I'. Being separate from what is seen is duality is it not? You asked, 'Who feels?' I answer, this mind. That's why this doubt is important for me. So few seekers manage to see through the psychological ego through this questioning. So while there is a metaphysical-sounding awareness to be looking for and seemingly identifying with, I need to address this contradiction instead of ignoring it.

S: There is nothing to get. 'I am' is a pointer that points away from the imaginary person and his story of suffering. There is no enlightenment to attain, and there is no one to attain it. There is no entity who is suffering, only the body can suffer, and the body takes care of itself. There is no separate awareness, no separate consciousness, no suffering person: all of that is purely imagination. All psychological suffering, all ideas of enlightenment, all ideas of a separate me, and a separate awareness are pure imagination.

You don't need anything at all. There are no real problems—it's all imagination. There is nothing to attain, nothing to avoid. All there is, is this. This is it. This nothing that is everything. Thoughts and stories are spinning around in circles and the thoughts and stories are believed to be real. See that it's all imagination, and your imaginary search for imaginary enlightenment comes to an end. And here you are as you've always been—just this.

You want to see through the ego: there's no ego. You want to know the truth: there's no truth. You want to be free: you were never bound. You want to... whatever you want does not exist. So you continue chasing your own conceptual tail looking for something that doesn't exist and you wonder why you're frustrated. Give it up and go wash the dishes, do something constructive. Chasing enlightenment, freedom, peace, true knowledge or happiness; whatever you're chasing, is a complete waste of time. See this now, or keep seeking for another five, ten, or twenty years and see it then.

There is no enlightenment, there is no ego, there is no personal suffering: it's all imagination. Stop chasing your imaginary tail and do something constructive with your time—right now.

116

Stuck on a Hamster Wheel

Question: I think your site and personal experiences pretty much wrap up my life story. The resonation with the truth found in the core of religions, the search, and the deepening of the search; discovering the non-dual philosophy, and the resonation with Advaita.

My seeking hasn't been going on for as long, but it did begin around the same time. I'm twenty-three years old, and feel that the intellectual understanding is there. I am that. But, how can I know? Is that question even applicable, if there is no me?

The questions remain even after the clear pointers from many Advaita teachers. Is there any hope? I really wouldn't mind the seeking ending now! Instead of going on for another twenty years, or not even finding that which I am. It seems like I'm stuck on a hamster wheel: all this seeking, but not getting anywhere. When the intellectual understanding was still maturing, it seemed like I was going somewhere, it was feeding my spiritual appetite, but there's only so far that the reading can go.

Stephen: Having studied Advaita and other religious philosophies, what have you learned, what do you know at this point?

Q: I've found a common thread pointing to the ineffable. It seems that in each tradition, the message is not shining fully though. The resonation with the core of the teachings is what has kept me intrigued. I've learned that these philosophies have always fallen short. It seems that they're all missing something, or that somewhere along the path, a direction changed. I have learned that to a greater or lesser degree these religions point at a truth present within all beings. I have learned that this truth cannot be restricted to one religion, and that any conceptual boundary around it seems to falls short. I have learned that the more I know about it, the harder it seems to talk about this with others. I've learned that it can be perceived from many different angles, yet it seems the perception is not it.

S: How will you know when your seeking is finished, what will you have found?

Q: I'm not quite sure how I will know when the seeking will fall off. I try not to hold expectations, but I do feel that there will be a surety of who I am, beyond an intellectual understanding. And I suppose that the falling off of psychological fear, anxiety will come with that understanding. Not that those things won't come up, but that I won't be attached to them. I feel that I will have found the 'peace that surpasses all understanding' this surety of who I am at heart beyond the mind's filter, peace—just overwhelming peace.

S: You said, 'I feel that I will have found the peace that surpasses all understanding, this surety of who I am at heart'. What are you? What is real about you? What is imagination? Of what about yourself can you be sure?

Q: It seems I am that which is prior to that sense of waking, where the thoughts and feelings proceed to rush in, followed by actions. It seems that what I am is so subtle that I (as the mind) lose it, or lose track of it. At times I feel like I'm an individual trapped in this body, unable to escape its vices, hating and loving it at the same time.

That which is real, in the sense of permanence, can only be that which the thoughts arise on. But I overlook it, or seemingly do, so I'm not sure. If what the teachers are saying about this is so clear, why can't I see it?

The thoughts and feelings and perceptions seem temporary, so in that sense you could equate them to imagination. Although they seem real as they arise, they always pass. It seems the only thing that stays with the arising and falling of these perceptions is the awareness of them. It seems when I go to sleep, or lose myself in some action, even this awareness of actions seems to fade and I disappear. But when something catches my attention (sudden noise, feeling, etc) it seems I reappear. It seems that identification with the things that arise on this awareness happens, but even the identifications must fade in sleep. So I say that I am that which these things arise on, but often I find myself identified with what arises.

S: Stop for a moment right now and notice the fact that you are aware of these words. Do you sense this witnessing presence that is here now? This simple witnessing presence is what you are. It is your essential nature.

You may travel down many different spiritual paths for another five, ten, or twenty years. The paths and experiences will change, but you will always be the same. You are that which is watching all thoughts, feelings, sensations, actions, and experiences. The first twenty-three years of your life have brought many changes and experiences, but you are the underlying constant. You have never changed. You are that which is aware of everything that comes and goes. You are this simple presence of awareness that has always been here.

Stop again now and just notice this presence of awareness. This is what you are regardless of what arises. You are always here and now witnessing the comings and goings. It is this simple.

117

You Are the 'Watching'—So Just Watch

Question: I have been a seeker for sometime now, and I don't how I got started with this seeking thing. I was sort of led from one thing to another and I found that I have become a seeker. I've been working with self-enquiry for about a month now, but I'm just getting frustrated with it. Although I know that I am unable to control my thoughts, feelings or experiences, and everything is just happening, I still feel I should be doing something to get the understanding.

And now, even though I don't want to continue with self-enquiry, i.e. I want to stay with the 'I am', the mind automatically starts doing enquiry. I feel I can get the understanding by staying with the 'I am'. I'm feeling really frustrated about what to do, how I should proceed, and if I should stay with the 'I am'. Please advise.

Stephen: You are the 'watching', so just watch. There's nothing to do. There's nothing to attain. There's nothing to overcome. Just watch. It is this simple. Everything else is more of the same: spinning in circles chasing your own tail. You are the 'watching,' so just watch.

118

Are Experiences Personal or Impersonal?

Question: Everything is okay here: peace and ease most of the time. When I am aware, e.g. listening to music, it's as if it's happening in my head—it's kind of a 'personal' center. Do you have any comments or experiences?

Stephen: I am sitting here listening to music right now, too. I'm noticing that the music is playing; thoughts, feelings, and emotions are arising in response to the song. I'm noticing that the music is happening. The listening is happening. The thoughts, feelings and emotions are happening. I'm noticing that all of this is simply happening. All of this that is happening is neither personal nor impersonal: it just is.

It is only when the thoughts 'I am listening, I am thinking, I am feeling' arise that the appearance of a personal experience arises. But the listening, thinking, and feeling are happening naturally on their own. The thought 'I am…' happens after the listening, thinking, and feeling. Listening, thinking, and feeling are neither personal nor impersonal experiences. The ideas of personal or impersonal experiences are based on the thought 'I am'. The thought 'I am' is the birth of the appearance of separation, and the birth of the appearance of a personal experience.

But does the thought 'I' actually create a separate, personal experience, or does it just appear so? If the thought and image of 'I' are believed to be a real, separate entity, then all sorts of experiences can be attributed to it: so-called personal or impersonal, and different perspectives and points of reference of this 'I'. But when the I-thought is seen to be just a thought, can any experience be labeled as personal or impersonal? Who is having a personal or impersonal experience if there is no I-thought?

When there is no I-thought or image, is there any perspective or reference point from which awareness, consciousness, or witnessing is happening? Everything is simply happening: by no one and to no one.

119

Years of Searching and Struggling Have Evaporated

Question: Hi, Stephen. I just wanted to drop you a note to say thank you for your willingness to talk with me and point me in the right direction. Since our talk, everything has become astonishingly simple and clear. Years of searching, practicing, reading, struggling, and on and on have just evaporated. I still love reading your site (and also John's, Bob's and Jean-Pierre's), but the sense of urgency and the sense of 'you get it and I don't' have completely disappeared. It all seems so absolutely clear.

Another interesting development has been my work with clients (I'm a counselor). Absolutely every problem that I see folks dealing with is a problem of believed thought. I used to spend a lot of time dealing with the content of thinking. Now I spend much more time helping clients see the *fact* of thought. As people become more aware of thought as the creator of their moment-to-moment experience, suffering decreases. Pointing them back to this open space of awareness/being-ness seems to have the effect of peeling thought off of their eyeballs so that it becomes another object to look at (like a lamp or bookshelf) rather than a lens to look through. Well, I certainly don't want to give the impression that everything just drops away, and people walk out without a care in the world, but they do seem to lighten up as they begin to see how thought is creating their experience moment to moment. They begin to take their thinking less seriously, and begin to not look as much in the direction of thought for answers to their problems. It seems that they get beyond their habitual thinking, and often something new will occur to them. Pointing people in the direction of seeing that we are all what is aware of thought rather than believing that thought is truth can be such a relief for people! It also saves me from getting involved in the story. When people begin to see thought as just thought, they can see each thought, in a sense, as a brick. The problem is that we all build houses out of the bricks and the houses look very real, but we forget that they're just made out of thought.

Again, Stephen, thank you very much for your work with me. This all fell into place when you said that your whole reason for sharing this had to do with ending psychological suffering. That really struck me, as did your unrelentingly simple and practical approach. I hope all is well with you and I hope we can stay in touch.

Stephen: Thank you for sharing. It's great to hear from you! Doesn't it feel good to share this with others? I think you may have struggled with this for years as I did, so now you speak from your heart and your own direct experience, and share the fact that it's possible to be free of psychological suffering.

Years of suffering can come to an abrupt halt, followed by laughter, tears and wonder when we see that all of our problems were imaginary. And that what we are is the Peace that we were struggling to attain by controlling our imaginary stories and the experience of the imaginary character called 'me'. Thank you for staying in touch and sharing your experience.

120

Ending Psychological Suffering is Shockingly Simple

Question: I have been reading the correspondence on your website, and would like to take up your kind offer of email contact. I have been pursuing the understanding of what 'Life, the Universe and Everything' is all about since I was fourteen (thirty-eight years ago), beginning with psychic phenomenon and moving through Hindu philosophy, J. Krishnamurti, Jean Klein, Nisargadatta, Tony Parsons etc. and many other teachers, including Bob Adamson.

In some ways my intellectual grasp of the message is, I think, fairly clear. And there is a sense that through the months and years it is becoming clearer. But psychological suffering persists. This is perhaps the main motivating force of the enquiry—a deep sense of loneliness, loss and worthlessness that has shaped and blighted the last forty years.

I know all the Advaita-speak that would qualify all the above personal expression into something more factual. I could counsel myself in a fairly convincing liberated non-person manner and analyze the component elements in a J. Krishnamurti-like style. I can talk the talk, but I don't walk the walk! This self sometimes longs for its own end and absence (another contradiction in terms I know). In the lyrics of a song 'I struggle like a fish caught on dry land' (having the idea of course that I am not a fish and there is no dry land). There does not seem the capability (whatever it may be) here to see first-hand the roots of this bondage and suffering and its ending. It seems I have largely understood all that I have read and heard about it, but at the core it has made little difference. And it feels like this just can't, and mustn't go on much longer. One point on which I stick is expressed in your correspondence entitled *Witness The Dissolution Of The I*. The questioner points out that any experience of awareness makes of it an object, which it is not. You agree, and then go on to say that 'once you know yourself as awareness...' But what is it that knows itself as awareness? What do you mean when you say this? Awareness, not being an object, has no qualities, therefore cannot be experienced.

Therefore it seems that this knowing is the knowing of an idea, the experience of a notion, a thought. Is this knowing merely the experience of a thought, an idea to the effect 'I am awareness'? It is so confusing. Not being clear myself, so much of what I read is taken on trust pending personal verification. Yet statements which appear to be meaningless once looked at closely undermine that trust and lead me to wonder if the whole thing is just a verbal con or another religious ideology which people follow due to lack of sufficient intelligence to see the contradictions inherent in the ideas presented. Please could you clarify?

Stephen: My interest in communicating this message is to share the fact that it's possible to be free of psychological suffering and spiritual seeking. I have no interest in proving the validity of any religious ideologies, understanding the nature of life, or unveiling the mysteries of the universe. I have no interest in proving anything at all to anyone at all. My approach is to share my direct experience, and to speak from the heart about what I have found to be true. And I am finding that those who stop for a moment, consider the suggestions offered, and apply them to their own direct experience are finding themselves free of psychological suffering. You may notice that the message being shared here is shockingly simple. And possibly for that reason, those who have keenly developed intellects tend to overlook the obvious, and continue exercising their intellect with never-ending questions, doubts, and 'Yes, buts!' So the appearance of suffering continues.

If you stop for a few moments and look to your own direct experience for the answers, you may be surprised how quickly and easily psychological suffering comes to an end. Let's consider the fundamental process of psychological suffering. Observing psychological suffering in your own direct experience, what do you notice about it? Isn't it true that psychological suffering is composed of thinking, imagination, and stories about 'me'? When there is no thinking, imagination, or stories about 'me', is there any psychological suffering at all? Is it possible to suffer psychologically without thought, imagination, and a story about 'me'?

So, isn't it obvious that all psychological suffering is thought-based and imaginary? If you are experiencing psychological suffering, you are imagining things—period, end of story. Do you see this? Freedom from psychological suffering is this simple. Nothing can trouble you but your own imagination.

Now, let's consider the fundamental fact of what you are in essence. Again, look to your own direct experience for your answer. Right now these words are being seen, thoughts are arising in response to these words, there is awareness of the room in which you're sitting, sounds are being heard, there is awareness of all that's happening in your experience right now. Do you notice that the content of awareness, or the objects of awareness are constantly changing? Sometimes there is awareness of thoughts, then feelings, then sensations, and then actions. Sometimes there is awareness of the body, and sometimes of the mind (the thinking process).

Right now notice the presence of this awareness. You are this awareness. If you are not here now as awareness, there can be no thoughts, no feelings, no sensations, no actions, no body, and no mind. Unless you are here now there can be no imagination, no story, no suffering, and no freedom from suffering. Without your presence as awareness there can be no intellect, no doubts, no questions, no answers, and no 'Yes, buts!'

Can anything exist for you if you are not aware? Can you exist if there is no awareness? So, isn't it clear that what you are in essence is this simple presence of awareness: and that all of your psychological suffering is based on thoughts and imaginary stories that are playing in you? If your interest is in being free of psychological suffering and spiritual seeking, then look to your own direct experience for answers to the fundamental questions posed here. It is this simple. The ending of psychological suffering and spiritual seeking does not require faith, trust, understanding of complex religious philosophies, or a keenly developed intellect. Psychological suffering and spiritual seeking come to an end by seeing in your own direct experience that what you are in essence is simply awareness, and that nothing can trouble you but imagination.

121

Where Does All of This Leave Me?

Question: I hope you don't mind me running more of a general observation rather than a question by you, although I really would like to hear your response.

What's struck me about this teaching is that if it really is so that there's no one here (and it is so, because the 'me' cannot be found except as fleeting thoughts), then there really is no free will (who would exercise it?) and there really is no where to go (who would go there?) and there really is nothing to do (who would do it?). Everything, absolutely everything, including the seeking, the frustration with seeking, the re-seeking, the abandonment of seeking, are all just happenings, happening to no one. Everything is as it is, it could be labeled perfect or good or bad, but in the end it is as it is. It could not be any other way. There is no one to re-direct the course of events, to choose a different path. No one wakes up, no one is dreaming, no one is liberated, no one self-enquires. If any of these things happen (to no one) then they happen completely spontaneously and cannot be worked toward (who would work toward it?).

Well, where does all of that leave me? Seemingly with absolutely nothing to do and nowhere to go! But then I never did anything anyway, so there's just the observation of things happening, sometimes intermingled with a belief (by no one) that I do things. There's nowhere to go with this is there? Or have I got it completely wrong?

Stephen: You're noticing that life is happening spontaneously, and there is no separate, controlling entity, no ego or me there in you. What you are in essence is this witnessing presence that is watching as life unfolds. Even the sense of ego, the sense of me, or I comes and goes spontaneously, and is witnessed as an appearance in awareness.

There is nothing to do, nowhere to go, nothing to accomplish, nothing to become. There is no 'me' who's living life. Life is happening. You're seeing the fundamental truth expressed by the statement, 'Consciousness is all there is, and I Am That.'